W9-ASO-717

Marguerite Yourcenar

Twayne's World Authors Series
French Literature

David O'Connell, Editor
University of Illinois at Chicago

TWAS 758

MARGUERITE YOURCENAR
(1903–   )
Photograph courtesy of Jacques Robert, N.R.F.

Marguerite Yourcenar

By Pierre L. Horn

Wright State University

Twayne Publishers • Boston

CARNEGIE LIBRARY
LIVINGSTONE COLLEGE
SALISBURY, N. C. 28144

Marguerite Yourcenar

Pierre L. Horn

Copyright © 1985 by G. K. Hall & Company
All Rights Reserved
Published by Twayne Publishers
A Division of G. K. Hall & Company
70 Lincoln Street
Boston, Massachusetts 02111

Book Production by Elizabeth Todesco
Book Design by Barbara Anderson

Printed on permanent/durable acid-free
paper and bound in the United States of
America.

Library of Congress Cataloging in Publication Data

Horn, Pierre L.
  Marguerite Yourcenar.

  (Twayne's world authors series.   French literature; TWAS 758)
  Bibliography: p. 111
  Includes index.
  1. Yourcenar, Marguerite—Criticism and interpretation.
I. Title. II. Series.
PQ2649.08Z69 1985   848'.91209   84–27889
ISBN 0–8057–6608–1

848.914
·Y81

A la mémoire de ma mère
A Mary Beth

117865

Contents

About the Author
Preface
Chronology

Chapter One
Biography of the First *Immortelle*   1

Chapter Two
Prose Fiction before *Mémoires d'Hadrien:*
Developing a Creator's Talent   8

Chapter Three
Mémoires d'Hadrien:
Meditations of a Roman Emperor   27

Chapter Four
L'Oeuvre au noir: A New Alchemy   43

Chapter Five
The Autobiographical Works   58

Chapter Six
Writings of Diverse Genres   72

Chapter Seven
Conclusion   96

Notes and References   99
Selected Bibliography   111
Index   118

About the Author

Pierre L. Horn was born in Paris, France, where he studied at the Lycée Voltaire. He received his B.A. from Brooklyn College and his M.A. and Ph.D. from Columbia University. A member of the Department of Modern Languages at Wright State University, Professor Horn has written numerous articles on nineteenth- and twentieth-century French literature, especially on the image of women in fiction and on women writers of the last fifty years. He is also coeditor of a collection of essays, *The Image of the Prostitute in Modern Literature*.

Dr. Horn was made a Chevalier dans l'Ordre des Palmes Académiques by the French government in 1978.

Preface

Despite publications dating back over more than sixty years—two works of poetry appeared in 1921 and 1922 when she was in her late teens—public recognition has been slow for Marguerite Yourcenar. This is due mainly to her uncompromising stylistic rigor, complex philosophical and ethical dilemmas, and a universal view that relies on Greek myths and figures: "this disciplined world . . . reaches through its heroes and its gods to the wondrous bestialities of our origins."[1] In addition, Yourcenar sees the immutability of time and space as challenging the complacent reader into posing the same hard questions found in Mediterranean and Eastern cultures. Today, however, her reputation is worldwide: books on the best-seller lists; translations into nineteen languages; scholarly interest and doctoral dissertations; awards, decorations, honorary degrees, and, of course, election to the French Academy as its first *immortelle.*

The present monograph examines Yourcenar's literary career which includes productions in all the major genres. Although most of them are successful with the critics and the readers, it is her novels that have brought her fame and financial security, especially after *Mémoires d'Hadrien* came out in 1951. The first chapter of this study briefly presents the highlights of her life, the eclectic education she received from her father, and the variety of her creation. Chapter 2 studies the prose fiction before 1951 and shows the development of recurring themes and characterizations, along with the elaboration of a narrative technique she would often favor.

The next two chapters deal with *Mémoires d'Hadrien* and *L'Oeuvre au noir.* Both masterpieces reveal her profound and passionate knowledge of human beings set against the background of history, but do not truly belong to the historical novel type. Chapter 5 gives insights into Yourcenar's inner self through the discussion of the prose poems of *Feux,* her autobiographical writings, and her oneiric tales. The last critical chapter analyzes her other works, that is, plays, poetry, translations, and essays, and clearly demonstrates the breadth of her intellectual and thematic interests.

Yourcenar declared to a *Figaro* interviewer that "for the writer, there is always the need to cry, even if it is in the wilderness, to express certain ideas which seem useful to him."[2] As long as there will be readers who want to discover how people, different from yet similar to themselves, are mirrored in literature and who want to explore the potential merit of other actions and world views, the vast oeuvre of Marguerite Yourcenar will remain an admirable fountainhead of daring thought and quiet wisdom.

For their support during the writing of this book I wish to extend my special thanks to the Wright State University Faculty Research Committee for their financial aid; Joy Iddings of the university library for her cheerful cooperation; Richard Calhoun of Academic Research Associates for his assistance in providing copies of hard-to-find articles; Professor David O'Connell for his editorial help; and my wife for the intelligence of her observations, her loving encouragement, and *parce que c'est elle.*

I am indebted to Mme Marguerite Yourcenar and to Editions Gallimard, Editions du Centurion, and Farrar, Straus & Giroux for their kind authorization to quote from her works in French and English, and to Indiana State University Press and *World Literature Today* and their editors for permission to cite material previously published under their imprints.

With the exception of *Alexis, Denier du rêve, Feux, Le Coup de grâce, Mémoires d'Hadrien, L'Oeuvre au noir,* and *Les Charités d'Alcippe et autre poëmes,* all translations are my own.

Pierre L. Horn

Wright State University

Chronology

1903   8 June, Marguerite Yourcenar born in Brussels, Belgium, to Michel de Crayencour and Fernande de Cartier de Marchienne. Ten days later her mother dies.

1912   Moves with her father from northern France to Paris.

1914   Goes to England and lives near Richmond.

1915   Returns to France.

1919   Privately educated, she passes her *baccalauréat* examinations at age sixteen in Nice.

1921   *Le Jardin des chimères* under the pen name Marguerite Yourcenar.

1922   *Les Dieux ne sont pas morts.*

1929–1931   Father dies. *Alexis ou le traité du vain combat* and *La Nouvelle Eurydice.* Travels to Switzerland, Italy, Greece, and lives on Aegean Sea island.

1932   *Pindare.*

1934   *La Mort conduit l'attelage* and *Denier du rêve.*

1936   *Feux.*

1937–1938   Several stays in the United States. *Nouvelles orientales* and *Les Songes et les sorts.* Translates Virginia Woolf's *The Waves.*

1939   *Le Coup de grâce.*

1940–1950   Part-time instructor of French and art history at Sarah Lawrence College (Bronxville, New York) and Hartford (Connecticut) Junior College. Articles and poems in various expatriate reviews. *La Petite Sirène,* adapted from the tale by Hans Christian Andersen, staged at the Wadsworth Athenaeum, Hartford (1942).

1947   Translates Henry James's *What Maisie Knew.* Becomes American citizen and changes her name legally.

1950   Moves to Mount Desert Island, Maine, with Grace Frick, her long-time friend and translator.

1951 *Mémoires d'Hadrien* awarded the Prix Fémina-Vacaresco.

1954 *Electre ou la chute des masques.*

1956 *Les Charités d'Alcippe et autres poëmes.*

1958 *Présentation critique de Constantin Cavafy* with translations of his poems (in collaboration with Constantin Dimaras).

1962 *Sous bénéfice d'inventaire* awarded the Prix Combat.

1963 *Le Mystère d'Alceste* and *Qui n'a pas son Minotaure?*

1964 *Fleuve profond, sombre rivière,* translations of Negro spirituals.

1968 *L'Oeuvre au noir* receives the Prix Fémina.

1969 *Présentation critique d'Hortense Flexner,* with translations of her poems.

1970 Elected to the Académie royale belge de Langue et de Littérature françaises.

1971 *Théâtre,* two volumes gathering her six plays.

1974 *Souvenirs pieux.*

1977 *Archives du Nord. Le Coup de grâce* made into a film by German director Volker Schlöndorff.

1979 *La Couronne et la lyre,* translations of ancient Greek poetry. Grace Frick dies.

1980 Decorated with the rank of *Officier* of the Legion of Honor. 6 March, elected to the French Academy. *Les Yeux ouverts,* interviews with Matthieu Galey.

1981 *Mishima ou la vision du Vide* and *Anna, soror . . .* (new version of "D'après Greco" in *La Mort conduit l'attelage*).

1982 *Comme l'eau qui coule* (new version of "D'après Rembrandt" in *La Mort conduit l'attelage,* plus *Anna, soror . . .*). Elected to the American Academy of Arts and Letters. *Oeuvres romanesques* published in the prestigious "Bibliothèque de la Pléiade" series.

1983 *Le Temps, ce grand sculpteur.* Translates James Baldwin's play *The Amen Corner.* Receives the Erasmus Prize.

1984 *Blues et gospels,* translations of black American lyrics.

Chapter One
Biography of the First *Immortelle*

Marguerite Yourcenar, the daughter of upper-class and aristocratic parents, was born on 8 June 1903 at 193 avenue Louise, a fashionable neighborhood of Brussels, Belgium. Her father, Michel de Crayencour, was of solid northern French stock with antecedents that can be traced to the early 1500s. He was a handsome and adventurous man who had sown his share of wild oats, including an adolescent fugue to Antwerp to embark as a cabin boy on any ship bound for China or Australia, enlistment in the French army with subsequent desertion to England where he became the lover of his lodger's wife, mutilation of his left middle finger to prove his unselfish devotion to her, and a cosmopolitan life spent in European spas and casino towns. [1]

Marguerite's mother, Fernande de Cartier de Marchienne, was the heiress of a long line of wealthy Belgian landowners and industrialists, the first of whom was governor of the city of Liège in 1366. She too had scandalously flouted the morality of her caste by going with her future husband on a "voyage de fiançailles" which took them both to Germany, followed after the wedding in 1900 by another two years of traveling through the continent of the Belle Epoque. [2] It was, therefore, quite by accident that Marguerite was born in the Belgian capital ("I merely happened to be born in Brussels")[3] as if between trains bound for Bordighera, Menton, or Vienna.

After her mother died of puerperal fever and peritonitis, the baby was raised by a series of women—half-maids, half-mistresses—for whom she alternately felt tenderness, admiration, respect, love, and benevolence. She was educated both by her father, who made her read aloud and in the original the great masterpieces of France, England, Greece, and Rome,[4] and by tutors who taught her non-literary subjects. Thanks to this private education young Marguerite was able to live in various places, first in Paris (1910–14), then in

1

Richmond, England, during the first year of World War I, and later on the French Riviera where at sixteen she successfully passed the *baccalauréat* qualifying examinations.

While still a teenager, Mlle de Crayencour published—at her father's expense—her first work in 1921, under the name of Marguerite Yourcenar. Although her pen name has a faintly Central European ring to it,[5] it is in fact an incomplete anagram of her patronymic. Done as much to create a persona separate and free from her real self—"as one takes a new name when entering the orders"[6]—as for the sheer fun of mystification,[7] this pseudonym became her legal name when she opted for American citizenship in 1947. *Le Jardin des chimères* presents in dialogue form a long poetic retelling of the Icarus legend and already announces several of the themes that will be developed in her later writings. The following year she published her first collection of poems, *Les Dieux ne sont pas morts*. Written mainly between her fourteenth and nineteenth years, it owes much to the symbolists, especially Maurice Maeterlinck, for its language and images and much to the Greeks for its subject matter.

Yourcenar and her father continued to travel to the fashionable European centers of gambling and horse-racing until his death in 1929, which is also the year of her first novel, *Alexis ou le traité du vain combat (Alexis)*, set in Central Europe. It was favorably reviewed in the press for the perspicacious analysis of the narrator's character and for the form the author would often thereafter employ—the confessional letter.

Now by herself, she toured Holland and Belgium, which she had not seen since her childhood, as well as Switzerland, Italy, Turkey, and Greece. There she lived for two years on a small island in the Aegean Sea and worked on her second book, *La Nouvelle Eurydice,* a short novel published by Bernard Grasset in 1931, which she acknowledges as being "less good" than the first.[8] Her essay on the Greek lyric poet Pindar in 1932 contains many useful comments and shows again the love and admiration for the Mediterranean world that remain constants of her life, as she continues to find inspiration in the sunny clarity of the great works and deeds of both ancient and modern artists and rulers.

La Mort conduit l'attelage (1934) is her next work. It comprises three short stories, each exemplifying the particular manner of a painter (Dürer, El Greco, Rembrandt), the first of which was later developed into the prize-winning *L'Oeuvre au noir*. That same year she also published *Denier du rêve (A Coin in Nine Hands*, dramatized as *Rendre à César* in 1961) which depicts the lives and struggles of several Italians during Mussolini's Fascist rule. *Feux (Fires*, 1936), written after watching the dawn come up behind the Parthenon and on board a ship off the Bosporus, is a series of new interpretations of ancient Hellenic myths and legends along with maximlike poems that are "the product of a love crisis."[9]

The following year Yourcenar visited the United States, a visit she would make several times in the next two years. Meanwhile, her collection of short stories dealing with events and people of the Near and Far East *(Nouvelles orientales),* her essays on the non-Freudian, nonpsychoanalytical architecture of dreams *(Les Songes et les sorts),* and her translation (with a fine preface) of Virginia Woolf's *The Waves*, all came out in 1938. Also in that year she began her next novel, *Le Coup de grâce (Coup de Grâce),* completing it in a few weeks that fall, perhaps under Ibsen's benevolent shade, for she wrote the book in the same room of the Hotel Tramontano in Sorrento where the Norwegian playwright composed his *Ghosts.* Set in the postwar Baltic region, it was well received by the critics when published in 1939, and was subsequently made into a movie in 1977 by Volker Schlöndorff, a German director of the new wave. Although the film was favorably reviewed (e.g., by Vincent Canby in the *New York Times,* 6 February 1978), Yourcenar did not like it at all.

When in 1939 she came to the United States for a lecture tour, she found herself unable to return to Nazi-occupied Europe. Remaining in this country, she contributed poetry and essays to various expatriate journals (especially to *Fontaine* in Algiers and *Les Lettres françaises* in Buenos Aires), and earned a modest living as part-time instructor of French literature and art history at Hartford Junior College and at Sarah Lawrence College in Bronxville, New York. She secured these positions, which she then held for ten years, upon the recommendation of English poet and critic Stephen Spender. It was also during World War II that her first play, *La Petite Sirène,* a *divertissement dramatique* based on the Hans Christian Andersen fairy tale, was produced and directed at the Wadsworth Athenaeum of Hartford, Connecticut, by Everett Austin, Jr.

It was during this period too that she started collecting and translating many of the Negro spirituals that would come out in book form only in 1964 under the poetic title of *Fleuve profond, sombre rivière.* In addition, she prepared a translation of Henry James's short novel, *What Maisie Knew,* that was published in 1947 by Laffont. Having decided to live permanently in the United States, she became a naturalized citizen in 1947, and three years later, after she had fallen in love with an island, "high and rocky, covered in its lower regions with evergreens and oak trees,"[10] Marguerite Yourcenar bought a small frame house with her long-time companion, friend, and co-translator, Grace Frick (a former teacher of English at Barnard College), and moved to Mount Desert Island, off the coast of Maine. She has lived there ever since, with frequent travels throughout the United States, Canada, Europe, and Asia.

When after the war she received a trunk from Switzerland containing family papers and trinkets left there for safekeeping, she also found the outline and beginning of the novel that would solidly establish her literary reputation and bring her more than mere *succès d'estime.* This first draft was to become *Mémoires d'Hadrien (Memoirs of Hadrian),* the fictional first-person narrative of the great second-century Roman emperor.[11] Published in 1951, it was extremely well received by the critics on both sides of the Atlantic and subsequently awarded the Prix Fémina-Vacaresco for best historical novel of the year.

Despite this acclaim, however, Marguerite Yourcenar did not become a household name. This is partly due to her remote residence and partly to her refusal to become a *lionne* of Paris literary circles. She much preferred to travel or to live in her little white house in the company of Grace Frick, Zoé, her cocker spaniel, and Joseph, a tamed gray-striped squirrel. Tending her garden, baking bread, speaking with her down east Yankee neighbors, fighting for environmental issues, and above all writing—plays (1954, 1961, 1963), poetry (1956), literary and historical essays (1958, 1962, 1964), and translations (1958, 1964) which appeared over the next thirteen years—occupied the majority of her time.

The publication of *L'Oeuvre au noir (The Abyss)* in 1968, though not changing her simple life much, brought her fame and recognition when it was selected in a unanimous first-ballot vote by the Fémina Jury for their prestigious prize and received worldwide notoriety (it was translated into eighteen languages). The novel recounts with a vividness reminiscent of Flemish painters the adventures of Zeno, a sixteenth-century humanist and universal man, as he crisscrosses Europe during the tumultuous era of the Reformation.

Honors were quick to follow: honorary degrees (Smith, Bowdoin, Colby, Harvard); election to the Académie royale belge de Langue et de Littérature françaises, where she replaced the late American literary historian, Benjamin M. Woodbridge, author of *Le Roman belge contemporain* (1930); literary prizes (Grand Prix de Monaco, Prix National des Lettres, Grand Prix de Littérature de l'Académie française). In the meantime, she published two volumes of her autobiography, *Souvenirs pieux* (1974) and *Archives du Nord* (1977). The first traces her maternal line and the second her father's; and, although Yourcenar hardly appears in the text, her presence permeates both books and gives the reader an excellent understanding of who and what the writer is, thinks, and feels. A more autobiographical third volume, *Quoi, l'Eternité?* (from an Arthur Rimbaud line), is currently in the revision stage.

The year 1979 brought sorrow as well as excitement to Marguerite Yourcenar. In November Grace Frick, her friend and collaborator of some forty years, died of Hodgkin's disease. But it was also the year when her candidacy for Roger Caillois's seat at the Académie française was being advanced by many admirers, including then President Valéry Giscard d'Estaing and academician Jean d'Ormesson. Members of the Academy quickly split into two groups: traditionalists rejected her on the grounds of her non-French birth (forgetting about Eugène Ionesco and about Julien Green's dual citizenship), her foreign nationality (by official application she regained her French status), and especially her sex (Yourcenar refused to budge on this objection!), whereas modernists focused on her talent, her works, and yes on her gender too, arguing that the time had finally arrived to choose a female member notwithstanding the fact that Mlle de Scudéry, Mme de La Fayette, Mme de Staël, George Sand, Anna de Noailles, and Colette were never so honored. After a stormy session followed by a three-month postponement, Marguerite Yourcenar received on 6 March 1980 twenty votes to Museum of Natural History Director Jean Dorst's twelve, and thus became the first woman elected to the French Academy since it was founded by Cardinal de Richelieu in 1635. Breaking further with tradition, she wore a long black velvet skirt and white blouse (and no sword) designed by Yves Saint-Laurent rather than the green and gold-embroidered uniform and cocked hat at the formal reception ceremony (22 January 1981).

Finally, her translations of ancient Greek poetry also came out in 1979 under the title *La Couronne et la lyre* and proved to be an instant success—both critical and financial—remaining on the best-seller list for fourteen weeks, to some extent as a result of the violent controversy and publicity surrounding her candidacy to the Palais Mazarin.

She has now been interviewed on French radio and television, discussed in scores of newspapers and magazines, including a long article in the 18 January 1981 issue of the *New York Times Magazine,* and decorated with the rank of *Officier* of the Legion of Honor. While she obviously enjoys the recognition she so richly deserves, Yourcenar still refuses to act the role of the celebrity and trailblazer. She continues to work simultaneously on several projects, including the publication of her complete works in the prestigious "Biblio-thèque de la Pléiade" (her *Oeuvres romanesques* was released in 1982), and has published a series of fascinating conversations with Matthieu Galey of *Magazine littéraire, L'Express* and *Les Nouvelles littéraires (Les Yeux ouverts),* an insightful monograph on the modern Japanese writer Yukio Mishima, *Mishima ou la vision du Vide,* both in 1980, plus new versions of the El Greco and Rembrandt short stories (from her 1934 *La Mort conduit l'attelage*) entitled *Comme l'eau qui coule* (1981–82). In late 1983 appeared her translations of five Mishima nō plays and of James Baldwin's *The Amen Corner;* also, many of her essays were collected and published as *Le Temps, ce grand sculpteur.* In addition, in 1983 the *Washington Post* reported that Yourcenar's name had been suggested for the Nobel Prize for Literature (the award went to British author William Golding).[12] Finally, *Blues et gospels,* translations of black American lyrics, came out in 1984.

Like Balzac, Flaubert, and Proust before her, Yourcenar views her characters as close members of her family, saying in one of many instances, "I love Zeno like a brother" (*SP,* 217); her imaginary creations are, for her, always worth quoting and using as sources of support and advice, as well as exemplars of proper conduct: "Not all our books will perish . . . ; some few men will think and work and feel as we have done, and I venture to count upon such con-tinuators, placed irregularly throughout the centuries, and upon this kind of intermittent immortality" (*M,* 293).

Serene in her old age, Marguerite Yourcenar is ready to face death with "open eyes" like her Roman emperor, comforted in the knowledge that a physician (Zeno) and a priest (the prior of the Franciscans) will be present at her death-bed (*Y*, 241).

Chapter Two

Prose Fiction before
Mémoires d'Hadrien:
Developing a Creator's Talent

Although Marguerite Yourcenar started her career by writing poetry (*Le Jardin des chimères* [1921] and *Les Dieux ne sont pas morts* [1922], to be discussed in a later chapter), she ultimately showed a greater affinity for prose fiction (i.e., novels and short stories) since it allowed her flexibility in developing character, theme, and plot. This also served as a means of testing established literary canons within what appears to be a very traditional mode. In the works preceding the publication of *Mémoires d'Hadrien* exist many of the ideas found in the 1951 novel, for instance, weakness and failure in a world that admires strength and power, characters rejecting conventional bonds and emotions as they try to assert their individuality, and political intrusions into human affairs.

To convey this view of the world, Yourcenar chose a first-person narrative style that was especially popular in the nineteenth and early twentieth centuries. Part memoir, part confession, and part confidence, this technique, which she calls "the portrait of a voice,"[1] offers the protagonist the greatest opportunity to express his thoughts, feelings, and reactions, unimpaired by authorial screens and interventions. It is her desire to present the truth as the *narrator* sees it, whether true or not, without commenting in any way, since a lie can be as self-revealing as a truth; it is also her wish to grant free rein to her creations, without judging their opinions or actions. Either they are free, in which case the reader can draw his own conclusions, or they are being manipulated for whatever purpose, in which case they become mere puppets entirely devoid of life.[2]

Alexis ou le traité du vain combat

Marguerite Yourcenar's first novel, *Alexis ou le traité du vain combat* (*Alexis, or The Treatise of Vain Struggle,* 1929), deals with the painful discovery by the narrator-hero of his true sexual feelings and his attempt at explaining—but not apologizing for—his preference for his own sex: "I am not foolish enough to hope that I shall be approved of; I do not even ask to be accepted. . . . I wish only to be understood" (*Al*, 18).

Alexis de Gera, born to an old impoverished aristocratic family of northern Bohemia, writes a long farewell letter to his wife, Monique, whom he greatly admires but is unable to love. Since he wants to be as complete, honest, and sincere as possible, he follows a chronological sequence, starting with his fatherless childhood days in the dilapidated house at Woroïno where life was always somewhat sad and sullen. There, shy, even timorous, surrounded by his mother, several sisters, and their girlfriends whom he viewed in a brotherly light, he felt neither sexual curiosity about nor desire for women as he intuitively suspected the brutality of physical love. Rather, he was taught a certain reverence for women with whom he shared a kindred weakness and purity.[3] Furthermore, his sickly condition, his love of beauty, his nervous sensitivity, his musical talent, all tended to foster in him homosexual leanings. Two years in a Pressburg *collège* only reinforced his repugnance for the vulgar pleasures and libidinous obsessions of his classmates. And then, one day, Alexis understood everything. By accident, almost by fatality, "on this particular morning, I encountered beauty . . ." (*Al*, 37).

Henceforth, he suffers from terrible feelings of guilt and horror, condemning himself for what he constantly qualifies as a disease, a fault, a sin, a momentary madness, a vice. Having discovered that he has a body, he often swears to God never to surrender to his forbidden temptations and yet he does, and when he does *not* it is more out of shyness than willpower. Because he now wants to escape this tendency, he moves to Vienna at the age of nineteen. In the Austrian capital he leads a miserable life, giving private music lessons and working as an accompanist in a theater, still struggling with his personal demons as he tries to remain pure for various lengths of time, once for an entire year. It ends, however, as the worst period of his life, since it is the soul and mind that are wounded rather than the body.

After he recovers from a grave illness, he realizes like André Gide's immoralist that the world is indeed beautiful and life worth living: "That day I had, by means of my entire body, which was astonished to live again, my second revelation of the beauty of the world. You

know what the first one was. . . . I wept at the idea that life was
so simple and would be so easy if we ourselves were simple enough
to accept it" (*Al*, 67–68). A distant relative, bent on marrying off
Alexis, introduces him to Monique, a rich, beautiful, and good
young woman for whom he feels more attachment and affection than
love. Unable to explain why the wedding night cannot take place
and hopeful that it might at last cure his homosexuality,[4] he marries
her on a rainy October day. Their life together is both difficult and
painful as he finds it increasingly harder to be a good husband until
her pregnancy relieves him of his marital duty. He is no longer
willing to fight against his leanings and, in a mixture of savage joy
and liberating hatred, he "nevertheless . . . much prefer[s] sin (if
that is what it is) to a denial of self which leads to self-destruction
["démence," *O*, 75]. . . . Not having known how to live according
to common morality, I endeavor at least to be in harmony with my
own . . ." (*Al*, 104–5). He is now confident that his attempt at
changing his nature is indeed useless (a realization that is already
evident in the book's subtitle, "The Treatise of Vain Struggle") and,
therefore, his only course of action is to go away: "With the utmost
humility, I ask you now to forgive me, not for leaving you, but for
having stayed so long" (*Al*, 105).

In his plea for Monique's indulgence toward his feelings and
actions, past and present, Alexis, as Maurice Delcroix points out,
questions not only the moral order which alone establishes criteria
of guilt and innocence,[5] but also an unhappy existence which is
based on sham and hypocrisy. Indeed, it is the scrupulous honesty,
this unflinching reverence for womanhood, this serene refusal of all
compromises, this need to live freely, in sum, his quest for ideal
purity, the dominant force of Alexis's personality, as well as his
conception of life itself, that lead him to acknowledge that "life has
made me what I am, the prisoner . . . of instincts which I did not
choose but to which I resign myself . . . " (*Al*, 104). Moreover,
in emphasizing the extreme closeness of pleasure and suffering (*Al*,
14), he announces other Yourcenar characters who, according to
Jean Blot, will not flinch at sacrificing the loved one in their pursuit
of pleasure.[6]

Whereas the German poet Rilke, especially in the *Notebooks of
Malte Laurids Brigge*, a "profound [and] moving work" (*Al*, xiii)[7]
exerted a great influence on Yourcenar's thought, more in the tone
taken by Alexis and in his hesitations at baring his soul than in the

subject matter, André Gide too played a certain role, mainly in the structure of her short novel. Like Ménalque's, Amyntas's, Corydon's, her hero's name is borrowed from the *Eclogues* of Vergil; her subtitle, "Le Traité du vain combat," recalls his own "Le Traité du vain désir." In addition, his open treatment of the homosexual theme[8] and his successful renewal of the classical "récit à la française" helped her in choosing these particular types of subject and form. Edmond Jaloux, one of her early admirers, writes in his review of *Alexis* that the book seems to be the preface of another and that the novel ends when the story begins.[9] In fact, Yourcenar has said that she often considered writing a "pendant" from the wife's point of view, but never did because in order to add substantially to Alexis's narrative, the author "would have had to refer herself to a later epoch of their lives, say ten or even twenty years later, at a time when, loving him still, she begins to judge him and also maybe to judge herself." This time lag was irreconcilable given Monique's own age in 1930: forty to Yourcenar's twenty-seven; "she would have been too old in comparison to me; we fell between two periods" (*Y, 69*). Perhaps she also remembered the purposely unfinished aspect of so many of Gide's works and felt that hers was a complete whole needing no additional touches.[10]

La Nouvelle Eurydice

Alexis having received some favorable critical notices, Yourcenar decided very self-consciously to write her second novel, using the same literary form: "It was not appropriate for this different subject, and I have produced an . . . infinitely failed book."[11] Critics too, like Pierre Audiat, were severe with the work; indeed, Edmond Jaloux was one of the few to have liked "this fine, serious and somewhat austere book."[12]

Again written in the first person, *La Nouvelle Eurydice* (The new Eurydice, 1931)—which echoes *La Nouvelle Héloïse*—presents also the theme of homosexuality, although the male-male-female triangle takes on here a greater importance, as will be seen shortly. (In *Alexis,* the other male does not appear since Alexis is concerned solely with the freedom to love whomever he wants.)

The twenty-two-year-old hero, Stanislas, tells how he loved Thérèse d'Olinsauve and apparently was loved by her, but without knowing it, while Emmanuel, Thérèse's strangely complacent husband and his best friend, dares not make a scene, leaves on a business trip, and thereby thrusts them into an unwanted intimacy. Stanislas's love for the young woman, whom he compares to a flower (a gladiola), to a madonna whose face wears "the pathetic shadow which one sees in the center of old paintings,"[13] to a vision "that partakes of the novel and of the dream" (N, 13), is not an updated form of the romantic idealization in the tradition of Victor Hugo or Lamartine. In fact, his Platonic feelings are far from being without a certain meanness, violence, even sadism: "I envied [Emmanuel's] ability to make her suffer" (N, 31). When he learns that she has fallen ill after spending the night outside his house, uselessly calling his name and knocking at his door, he quite selfishly and resentfully blames her for not having tried harder and, especially, for making him wait in vain for her and thus endure so much mental—let alone sexual—desire and pain: "My grief, my self-denial could not have been: it seemed absurd that they ever were" (N, 126).

Furthermore, he is also torn by his attraction for Emmanuel, for whom he has always felt "a cult and a passion together" (N, 10); this is why he can easily wonder whether, in loving the wife, it is not the husband he really loves (N, 51). That the feeling is mutual is intimated at the end of the narrative and leads to d'Olinsauve's melancholia and suicide, not without Stanislas's relief at being rid of the terrible "burden of loving somebody" (N, 224).

After Thérèse has died of pneumonia, he, like a modern Orpheus, searches for her grave, yet is almost filled with joy at the realization that he will never find it. When the d'Olinsauves' former maid reveals to him that Thérèse had in fact loved him, he declares, "Should I admit it? I was disappointed" (N, 113), not for being unworthy of her love but because she had in this fashion tarnished her image in his eyes.

What makes this work so fascinating is not so much the further development of the theme of destruction of the loved one or a more complex analysis of homosexual love, but the multiple mystery present in the various relationships. Did Thérèse, as Jean Blot asks, love Stanislas because Emmanuel loved him? Did Emmanuel love Stanislas the more because Thérèse loved him also or did he love Thérèse only?[14] While the village priest considers them the happiest of couples, Mlle Armance, his sister, seems to claim that Thérèse had lovers and was the talk of the region, and the maid raises the question of Emmanuel's conduct and how brave Thérèse was in not leaving him. So many prismatic facets cannot be visualized all at once since no one participant knows the entire truth, and even the apparently meticulous reconstruction attempted by Stanislas sheds little, if any, light on the couple's secrets. The Greek Eurydice died and disappeared back into the netherworld as soon as her husband turned to look at her, leaving behind but the reflection of her shadow, and Yourcenar's heroine, too, vanishes because Stanislas, more interested in the idea of happiness than in being happy, had "sought the possession of the mind, more futile than that of the body" (*N*, 239). All that is left, therefore, is the oppressive malaise that once again Fate has dealt harshly with the three characters, for in the end "we are all actors: we play a role which, besides, we do not choose . . . " (*N*, 198). Unlike Alexis, who willingly and neatly assumes control of his existence, Stanislas prefers the vague, blurred, gray monotony of a life endured. And he rushes back to his room before nightfall.

Marguerite Yourcenar's next work, a collection of three short stories published in 1934 under the general title of *La Mort conduit l'attelage,* has been for the most part completely rewritten and released in 1981–82 with the new title of *Comme l'eau qui coule,* and one of the stories became the novel, *L'Oeuvre au noir.* This 1968 work is the subject of chapter 4, while the other two stories will be more usefully discussed in chapter 6.

Denier du rêve

While *Denier du rêve* (recently translated into English as the less poetic *A Coin in Nine Hands*) was first published in 1934, it was, according to Yourcenar's own preface,[15] considerably reworked in a subsequent edition (1959), and its "definitive version" is dated 1971. However, because "the characters, the names, the personalities, the relationships, and the settings remained the same" and because "the main and secondary themes of the book, its structure . . . have also not changed" (*C*, 169), there is no need to consider *Denier du rêve* later in our study.

The story, set in 1933 in Fascist Rome, the eleventh year of Mussolini's dictatorship, centers around the activities of a few young Italians plotting to assassinate the Duce. Yourcenar describes the lives and dreams of the protagonists, whether they are involved in the conspiracy or not, in the sober manner of a *tragedia dell'arte* (her phrase). Indeed, the novel follows rigorously the classical rule of the three unities: through the conventional device of a ten-lire coin passing from hand to hand we have the unity of action, this action occurring in one place, the Eternal City, and all happening within less than twenty-four hours. [16]

In re-creating the ambience of Mussolini's capital, "the hollow reality behind the bloated façade of Fascism" (*C*, 173), the author portrays characters who now live with the knowledge that they have lost their liberty, their vitality, the reassuring illusion of possible change. Too preoccupied to hide their own distress, too proud to act differently, they lock themselves behind solitary walls, living as strangers to each other. In addition, since Yourcenar wants to present in her works eternal conflicts and situations, many of these characters serve as mythic actors in a modern historical tragedy, uneasily balancing between the world of reality and the world of dreams.

Paolo Farina, a young lawyer whose wife (the future movie star, Angiola Fidès) has run off with a second-rate opera singer, offers a gift of a brand-new coin to Lina Chiari, his mistress. Since she has breast cancer, her best friend, Massimo Iacovleff, advises her to consult Dr. Alessandro Sarte, who recommends radical surgery. In an understandable surge of self-pity, she wants to hide her extremely pale face by making it again "vivante, intensément actuelle" ("lively, passionate" [*C*, 15]) through the use of a red lipstick she buys and pays for with the silver piece.

Giulio Lovisi, unhappily married and unsuccessful in his cosmetics business, accused by his wife of lusting after his shop assistant, Miss Jones, is a supporter of law and order and of the Catholic religion; he is also the father-in-law of Carlo Stevo, imprisoned on a penal island off the coast of Sicily for crimes against the state. He gives the ten lire to Rosalia di Credo for candles he lights to accompany his prayers to the Virgin Mary. Rosalia, whose dreams are forever fixed in Gemara, her ruined country estate in Sicily, and on her sister Angiola (for whom she had incestuous feelings), buys hot coals from Marcella Sarte with her coin. When her apartment catches on fire, she lets it burn because "she wanted to die" and also because she is unwilling and unable to fight against the wonderfully bittersweet "deadly seasickness" (*C*, 58).

An ardent anti-Fascist still married to, but separated from, her fashionable physician-husband, Alessandro Sarte, in whom she hates the "wealth, success, pleasure, happiness itself" (*C,* 63), Marcella loves Platonically, intellectually, almost abstractly, Carlo Stevo, whom she greatly admires for his talent, and lives in bliss with young Massimo. In a rare conversation with her estranged husband, she learns that during her years of political involvement she was being protected from the police through his connections; that Stevo has died in prison after divulging several names; that Iacovleff is a double agent; and, finally, that she still loves Alessandro, a feeling she is ashamed of and angry for. For her part, she tells her husband that she will try to kill Mussolini that same evening during a speech. Realizing that she has "stolen" from him the gun she will use, she hands Alessandro some money, and soon after he leaves she goes off to the Balbo Palace.

To escape the rain, Sarte enters a movie theater and, in a series of audacious gestures, makes love to Angiola, who is there also because she had wanted to see one of her movies. An *Anadyomene Venus* (*C,* 159), Angiola Fidès the actress appears to men to be the fantastic projection of erotic sensuality. In her celluloid image they find the fleeting pleasure of passion. She, too, finds in her life, on screen and off, compensation for the poverty and unhappiness of her youth, for the many humiliations received at the hands of strangers and loved ones alike. Her movie persona, however, has somehow become a rival who has robbed her of her life blood, of her very essence: "She was facing a vampire: this pale monster had drunk Angiola's blood. . . . She had sacrificed everything to this ubiquitous ghost. . . . When she died, she would try to imitate one of Angiola's deaths. . . . [Like a great feminine] Narcissus at the edge of luminous waves, she looked for herself in Angiola Fidès's reflection, in vain" (*C,* 105–6). Her only victory over the mirror self[17] takes place when this stranger in the movie theater makes love to her—Angiola the *woman*—a short-lived victory to be sure since the film is over in a few minutes (as is, one may note, the sex act itself) and she will have again and again to fight for her identity, so unable is she to stop playing a role. She cannot know, of course, the lasting impression she made many years before on an elderly French painter for whom she appeared nude ("a little Venus emerging from the waves" [*C,* 151]). Although she has long since grown to maturity, his memory of her as a young girl, with the light playing on her body, has remained, recurring here and there in all his paintings. Even as he approaches death he evokes once more this beautiful image, observing to Massimo that such are the "things that help when your time to die has come" (C, 152).

After the movie, Dr. Sarte buys Angiola a bunch of roses. A friend informs him that his wife has failed in her assassination attempt and has been killed: "A damp strand of hair snakes along the cheek of this dead Medusa [with] her eyes, wide open but blind . . . " (C, 118).[18] Marcella is a Medusa, destroyed not by a heroic and dashing Perseus but bludgeoned to death by a militia gone wild, as well as an Electra, avenging her dead father, whose brilliant ideas the Duce stole. In fact, she is viewed by all in a different light: by Yourcenar as the Sibyl, turned toward the future and knowing all too well that violent political action is the only recourse left to her fellow Italians; by Carlo Stevo as the incarnation of the People, angry at the cynical corruption of socialist ideals (C, 63–64); by Massimo Iacovleff as a Judith or a Charlotte Corday, intent on killing a tyrant who murders and enslaves (C, 88, 90), or as a Nemesis relentlessly pursuing the criminal with punishment (C, 91), an association also made with a museum painting entitled The Sleeping Fury (C, 159). Naturally, Marcella exemplifies all these righteous justice-seekers, and yet her unsuccessful act represents something more: an archetypal need to eradicate the father figure symbolized by Mussolini. That "the Chief of State," "Him," "the dictator," "the great man," "Caesar," as he is alternately called, is identified only by titles, that he never assumes a concrete presence in the novel, and that he is referred to in terms of his clothes[19] or stature—all have the effect of bestowing on him larger-than-life godlike characteristics, further emphasized by omnipresent propaganda posters and graffiti and by newsreels which forever watch, know, threaten. Actually, he does appear once, very quickly, at the end, to ironically underscore the uselessness of revolt against such a grandiose archetype created as much by fiction and illusion as by popular needs and vanities.

Marcella's commitment is a means of escaping from her nightmare and ultimately of acquiring, in the face of insurmountable odds, a presence—an existence—while at the same time granting her the death she subconsciously desires: "You want to kill Caesar," Massimo perspicaciously tells her, "but especially Alessandro, and me, and yourself. . . . Cleanse the spot. . . . Leave the nightmare behind. . . . Shoot, as in a theater, to bring down the set behind the smoke. . . . To be done with these people who are not real" (*C,* 89), to achieve what her husband calls the "orgasme de mourir" (*O,* 246; "culmination of death" [*C,* 113]). It is this irreconcilable conflict within her between the absurdity of life in search of a meaning and the wonderful attraction of death itself that forces Marcella to transcend her limitations and become a tragic heroine.

Dida, the flower merchant who received the coin from Alessandro Sarte, is a crafty old woman who denies her children and herself out of peasant cupidity and stinginess. She finds warming comfort in the sole possession of cold cash which she carries in a pouch around her neck like a talisman. She is, though, solid and strong: flowers (in her youth), tree trunks (now), gnarled hands, branches, feet rooted to the ground, November leaves (*C,* 119), these are some of the comparisons used to describe this old woman, with her superstitions and common sense, her lack of political knowledge and understanding of political realities, her narrow-minded provincialism and sophisticated openness, her meanness and compassion. In brief, like the Earth she came from and finally symbolizes, she has a life force that will endure all and survive: "She was hard as the earth, eager like a root seeking sustenance, choking weaker roots . . ., stormy and sly as water" (*C,* 125). Still, despite her avarice, to ward off Father Cicca's terrible prediction, she hands quite ostentatiously the ten lire to what she takes to be a panhandler. This man turns out to be a well-known French painter, Clément Roux, mistaken for a beggar because of his drenched clothes and haggard appearance.

Roux has actually suffered a heart seizure and is kindly rescued by Massimo Iacovleff. Together, they slowly walk around the city at night, a walk that for both amounts to an epic descent into Hell (which Massimo qualifies as "a pitiful funeral vigil" [*C,* 153]) and provides them with the opportunity to reveal important secrets to each other and especially to themselves. Tired and despondent, Clément Roux throws the coin in the Fountain of Trevi, not so much to wish for a return to Rome as to wish for life, youth, and purity. Massimo, on the other hand, wishes that Roux had offered him the coin, for he will now need money to leave Italy.

Who is this Massimo, son of Russian exiles, humiliated student turned *agent provocateur* out of self-hate and expediency, half-friend, half-lover of Carlo Stevo? Yourcenar associates him with Thanatos

(*Y,* 86), the beautiful god of Death, since his touch is fatal to all his friends and acquaintances: Lina, Carlo, Marcella. Even Roux, who was given the obolus required for his crossing of the River Styx, takes Iacovleff for a thief of "great beauty" (*C,* 137) who happens to know his name and face. Massimo calls himself "the angel of the last hours" (*C,* 141), whom everyone loves. Although he never receives the *denier,* money too has corrupted his soul since, like another Judas, he has betrayed his friend and co-conspirator to the regime: "The loved disciple is . . . the one who hanged himself with thirty pieces of silver in his pocket" (*C,* 90).

After Roux and Massimo go their separate ways, in the early hours of the morning a water company worker, Oreste Marinunzi (also Dida's son-in-law), gathers up the change, among which is the *denier,* from the Trevi Fountain and with it drinks himself into a stupor in an all-night café. This same chapter provides a final view of each of the characters. Paolo Farina snores in his ship cabin on his return from Sicily; Mussolini sleeps the sleep of the just in his palatial bed; the Lovisis, unaware of Carlo Stevo's death, plan for his expected release; Dr. Sarte tells the authorities about his wife's last months; Lina Chiari dreams of Massimo; Clément Roux sleeps calmly in his hotel room; Angiola sleeps in Angiola Fidès's bed; Miss Jones, who missed her train, has slept badly in a flophouse and now anxiously awaits her departure for England; Dida sleeps in the courtyard of the Conti Palace; and, after packing his suitcase, exhausted, Massimo falls asleep at his table. The city also, with its fine museums and art galleries and Roman ruins, is fast asleep.[20]

It is appropriate that the novel end with Oreste Marinunzi in the guise of Bacchus. Ironically, everything seems to predestine him to a teetotaler's existence, from his last name with its sea etymology to his job as water-works repairman; even the coins he picked up were found in a water fountain at the foot of Neptune's statue. Thanks to the wine, his lot in life so improves that by the second bottle he has murdered with great pleasure his mother-in-law, almost out of a sense of justice and of righting a great wrong (much like his ancient Greek namesake) and told off his boss, and by the third bottle all his enemies have disappeared, he has quit his job, and having become the exemplar of the perfect demagogue, he has "doubled salaries, lowered the cost of living, won a war, and earned his place in the sun forever" (*C,* 166). Whereas the other characters have all tried to run away from their self-deception and achieved little, if anything, of their dream, Oreste Marinunzi may be the only one to find happiness and euphoria in the festive escape of alcohol and politics—"and [he] lay there, happy as a dead man" (*C,* 167).

Some of the novel's narrative techniques reveal the influence of William Faulkner and Virginia Woolf, particularly in such masterful scenes as Rosalia's flashback evocation of an idealized Gemara and its soul-wrenching destruction (*C,* 36–58) and the Vespers service at St. Mary Minor's Church, where by coincidence several characters have come in order to pray for special favors. Concerned only with his own thoughts and worries, each focuses on one metaphor used to describe the Virgin Mary (*C,* 27–29): "House of Gold" recalls for Rosalia her six-hundred-year-old estate; "Queen of Martyrs . . . Queen of Heaven" are the two facets of Marcella's assassination attempt—death or prison (*Regina Coeli* is a Roman jail); Clément Roux remembers a wonderfully beautiful girl when he hears "Ivory Tower," while with "Chosen Vessel" Lovisi realizes he forgot to buy his granddaughter's medicine; and Miss Jones upon hearing "Queen of Virgins" is reminded of the vulgar scene made by her employer's unjustly suspicious wife. The final "Orapronobis" mumbled together in one word summarizes well the illusion of their prayers, for it has become one more empty formula, as devoid of meaning as crowd noises on the stage ("rubarbara . . . barbararu . . . bararubar . . . rarubarba" [*C,* 143]) or political slogans.

Denier du rêve is a fascinating psychological puzzle whose pieces—the characters—can be considered from so many different angles that the whole, as in real life, can never be fully assembled or understood: "We are all shreds of material, faded rags, a mixture of compromises," declares Massimo all too lucidly (*C,* 90). Although these individuals, who are forever seeking affirmation of their being in an indifferent world are no more than fragile bits of matter, it is ironic that they themselves define and fashion that world by their own conduct and compromises. And life, itself so simple, becomes obscured by the very complexity of their particular natures; whether or not each recognizes it, the only true reality, the only permanence in an ephemeral world, is found in the unchanging nature of dreams. Thus, as the coin of the title travels from the hand of one dreamer to the next, we come to understand the Montaigne sentence Yourcenar uses for her epigraph: "To abandon one's life for a dream is to know its true worth."[21]

Nouvelles orientales

Most of Yourcenar's short stories were first published in various French reviews and then collected under the general title of *Nouvelles orientales* (Oriental short stories, 1938) in a literary series edited by Paul Morand for the Librairie Gallimard. Three other tales came out in 1962 and a fourth in March 1978, all ten included in the definitive edition released that year.[22] The adjective "oriental" should be taken in its largest sense, as in Victor Hugo's 1829 *Les Orientales*, considering that, although three stories are set in China, Japan, and India, six take place in Greece or the Balkans and one, "La Tristesse de Cornélius Berg," occurs in seventeenth-century Holland; of the latter, Yourcenar says it is included in order to give a view of art different from that found in "Comment Wang-Fô fut sauvé" (*O*, 1216).

All the stories deal in some way with an aspect of the fantastic or the imaginary. This is particularly true of "How Wang-Fô Was Saved" from a horrible punishment. The old Chinese painter, having aroused the emperor's wrath and hatred by his beautiful silk paintings which have no connection with the real world—"a mass of confused stains" (*O*, 1145)—and by his being truly loved and revered by his pupil, is condemned but first must complete an unfinished seascape. Wang's creative power is so strong that the painting's waters invade the throne room, and he and his devoted disciple climb into a bark and disappear forever "on this sea of blue jade which Wang-Fô had just invented" (*O*, 1149). Art, therefore, provides the artist with a metaphorical escape from the ugliness of reality and the transient quality of things. No such serene salvation exists in "The Sadness of Cornelius Berg," however. His portraits reveal to him the meanness of the human soul, his still lifes the ineluctable decay of matter, and his landscapes the fleeting nature of time. Echoing his relative's "God is the painter of the universe," Berg adds somewhat bitterly, "How unfortunate . . . that God did not limit himself to painting landscapes" (*O*, 1214).

Love, naturally, is another important theme treated in Yourcenar's tales. In one, Marko, an anti-Turkish Christian patriot, is captured and plays dead to avoid being killed. Despite tortures demanded by his jilted Moslem mistress to thwart his ruse, he remains totally immobile until she asks several young girls to dance before him. At such a sensual spectacle he cannot help but smile (one of the dancers quickly covers his mouth with her handkerchief), and it is his happy reaction which allows the narrator to express the tale's essence: "What . . . touches me is this exquisite euphemism, this smile on the lips of a victim for whom desire is the sweetest torture" ("Le Sourire de Marko" [Marko's smile], *0, 1156*). This joyful eroticism is missing from "Le Dernier Amour du Prince Genghi" (The last love of Prince Genghi) and replaced by the acrid bitterness of tears. The famous Japanese seducer, created by Lady Murasaki, is now old and blind and remembers sadly the wonderful mistresses of his youth but, incredibly, overlooks the most loving and faithful of them all. Another form of love is illustrated in "The Man Who Loved the Nereids" and who, although he is struck mute, blind, and simple as a result, nevertheless has revealed to him "the intoxication of the unknown, the exhaustion of miracle, the sparkling malignancies of happiness" (*0, 1182*), quite the opposite conclusion reached by the wise man in "Kali Beheaded": "Desire has taught you the inanity of desire; regret teaches you the uselessness of regret" (*0, 1206*).

Another tale, "La Veuve Aphrodissia" (The widow Aphrodissia), relates the story of Aphrodissia and Kostis the Red, her lover and her husband's murderer. When, six years later, Kostis is finally caught and beheaded and Aphrodissia secretly goes to see his corpse to mourn her loss, she notices her name tatooed on his arm. Terrified that she will be found out and stoned, she buries his body in a grave and, not unlike Mathilde de la Mole, she too flees with the severed head but ends by plunging over a precipice. Kostis is described as a big mass of red (hence his nickname) from his red hair and red jacket worn to buy horses to his enemies' spilled blood, and his own round head smeared with blood, all serving to make him the symbol for the setting sun at his chariot. Aphrodissia, dressed in her black widow's weeds, constantly reminded by others of her widowhood (even the title of the short story was changed by Yourcenar from "The Red Chief" to "The Widow Aphrodissia"), and compared to a "black mole" with its double connotation of night (blackness and blindness) is, on the other hand, the incarnation of Night come to steal the setting Sun (in fact, at the end, she is mistaken for a thief). In view of this, it is understandable that the sun should try to stop her progress by relentlessly beating down on her ("the air burned like a white-hot iron, and Aphrodissia pulled her shawl over her forehead, for it was essential not to be struck

down by heat before she had concluded her task" [*O*, 1199]). After
her theft of the head, the sun causes her to slip and fall to her death:
"The path [became] more and more slippery, as if the blood of the
sun, ready to set, had made the stones sticky" (*O*, 1200). Yourcenar
calls this confrontation "the night taking away the setting sun."[23]
In similar mythic fashion, the weak and pitiful old man with no
name is the fatidic Mysterious Stranger who brings to the banquet
host his appointed death in "La Fin de Marko Kralievitch" (The
end of Marko Kralievitch).

"Notre-Dame-des-Hirondelles" (Our Lady of the Swallows), in
addition to being the author's "personal fantasy . . . born of the
desire to explain the charming name of a little church in the Attic
countryside" (*O*, 1216), is concerned with the conflict between an
unyielding Christianity and a tolerant paganism. Out of religious
fervor, the monk Therapion wants to destroy the nymphs who live
in a cave high above his village and who present dangerous temptations to simple souls. To accomplish his mission, he builds a
chapel in front of their cave to prevent their escape and ultimately
bring about their death. The Virgin Mary herself intervenes, ad-
monishing the too zealous monk that God loves nymphs also and
that He created both Diana and Apollo. Finally, she "reconcile[s]
the life of the nymphs with the salvation of [Therapion's] congre-
gation" (*O*, 1191) by transforming the nymphs into swallows and
giving them shelter in her church.

Unfortunately, divine help appears too late for the poor young
wife and mother who is walled alive in a tower so that her body
will become part of the cement required to keep it standing. However, she is allowed to breastfeed her baby through an opening in
the brickwork until the child is weaned. The infant's life, therefore,
is preserved and allowed to blossom thanks to "the miraculous
spouting" ("Le Lait de la mort" [The milk of death], *O*, 1166) which
is the result of "the encounter between love and death."[24] In transcending her suffering, the heroine of this Poesque story is able to
prove that motherhood can be even stronger than death.

With *Nouvelles orientales* Marguerite Yourcenar uses what is for
her a new literary genre and adapts it to the style she has come to
favor, that of a narrator telling a story within a story. While, as
Jean Blot remarks, the *nouvelle à cadre* appears artificial and forced,[25]
it allows the writer to remain detached from the actual recounting

and at the same time to give the necessary omniscient corroboration to these fine old legends.

Le Coup de grâce

If, as has often been shown, the romantic hero is a man of refusal, required to live in a rigid society but rejecting its moral strictures, Eric von Lhomond, the first-person narrator of *Coup de Grâce* (1939)—by his aristocratic upbringing, his ethnic origins (half-German, half-Balt with some French blood), and his psychology—will demand from life the ideal, even harsh, purity of love as well as courage and self-sacrifice. "Why is it that women fall in love with the very men who are destined otherwise, and who accordingly must repulse them, or else deny their own nature?,"[26] asks Eric. Of this misunderstanding, writes Henri Hell, is born the tragedy befalling the three principal protagonists of this short work.[27] John Charpentier, writing in *Mercure de France,* believes he is not "exaggerating" when he calls *Le Coup de grâce* a "masterpiece."[28]

Von Lhomond, wounded in the Spanish Civil War where he fought on Franco's side, tells his twenty-year-old story while waiting to be repatriated to Germany. The action takes place after the Russian Revolution, during the anti-Bolshevik fighting conducted in the Baltic countries, especially in Courland (Latvia), by White Russians and other counterrevolutionaries. After several years' absence, Eric returns as a volunteer fighter with the counterrevolutionaries to the Castle of Kratovitsy, where live Conrad de Reval, a distant cousin and friend from adolescence, and Conrad's sister Sophie, who falls in love with him. However, he responds with a distance that only fans her passion: "What was ludicrous in the whole affair was this: it was my coldness and unresponsiveness that had won her" (*CG,* 37). To conquer Eric she will do anything up to and including self-abasement. The clear and useless advances of the beginning are followed by complete submission and gift of both the soul and the flesh, then revolt, and finally a defiance that leads her to a despondent series of casual encounters with other men until she discovers Eric's secret and, wounded in her body and heart, she joins the Reds against her own class.

Coup de Grâce, though, is not solely a poignant story of unrequited love, for Eric's coldness is caused mainly by his homosexuality and complicated by the passionate feeling he has always had for Conrad, "the one being . . . to whom I felt myself bound by a kind of pact" (*CG*, 59). His homosexuality is here reinforced by a pleasurable perversity and cruelty as he encourages and rejects in turn the young woman's attentions and favors: "Between Sophie and me an intimacy swiftly sprang up like that between victim and executioner" (*bourreau*) (*CG*, 33)—a simile he strikes again when he refers to her as a wounded bird and when he compares her to "un fruit . . . également [pour] la bouche et [pour] le couteau" (*O*, 104; "a fruit . . . ripe for the cutting, or consuming" [*CG*, 41]). Even his ambivalent shows of tenderness grate on her overwrought nerves as she feels his contempt for her: "She reopened her eyes . . . and read in my aspect something harder to bear, doubtless, than hatred or terror, for she recoiled, covering her face with her upraised arm . . . and that was the last time I ever saw her actually cry" (*CG*, 77). This constant seesawing motion between love and hate works to the same result, that is, "to make her love and suffer even more" (*CG*, 41), so that at the end of the novel, when she is taken prisoner, Eric is willing (albeit after a night of hesitation) to grant her last wish: to be shot by his hand. This is, of course, the *coup de grâce* of the title.

In Eric's narration, Conrad is portrayed throughout as having an attitude of correct aloofness. As a matter of fact, he remains a shadowy figure, the quintessential epitome of grandiose, youthful love and the embodiment of a period of life that has marked Eric greatly and represents for him "happiness, the real thing, the inalterable gold piece . . ." (*CG*, 14). Resembling in death Rembrandt's *The Polish Rider* (*CG*, 127), Conrad is divinely handsome, soft, pure, intolerant, fearless in danger; his pallor and frailness make him appear almost feminine, yet with the solidity of "a fixed point, a center, a heart" (*CG*, 10). Yourcenar attributes the narrator's reticence to unbosom himself about his friend to Eric's own reserve and tact, a *noblesse oblige* that prevents him from sharing with indifferent strangers his innermost feelings (*CG*, vii). There exists no such restriction in his retelling of the relationship with Sophie, perhaps because, in looking back, he cannot but admire and respect a true equal in the certainty with which she viewed people, events, and the world, gallantly pursuing to the bitter end the passionate dream that would absolve her of her sins.

Wrongly believing that Eric enjoys the company of loose women Sophie becomes sexually promiscuous, sleeping with all the soldiers billeted in the castle, taking up with Volkmar (a rival officer particularly despised by Eric)—more, it is true, to make him jealous than out of love for this other officer—and purposely drinking herself into a disgusting state out of despair. She remains good and basically pure despite her need to be battered and debased in Eric's eyes, as if she wanted to rid herself of the anguish of a woman caught in a world of men. A young woman in love, she is trying to fight back against the loved one's disinterest in the most effective manner she can, that is, by devaluing her own body and sex, in an attempt to persuade him that she must not be considered an inconsequential object,[29] through an orgy of sex. She does her very best (or worst) to prove to Eric that she is in fact worthy of his love, and her immediate failure ("an examination she had failed to pass" [*CG,* 69]) is due to his incapability of dealing with such a strong, aggressive woman. Unlike the willing and passive person we imagine *Alexis*'s Monique to be, Sophie refuses to be sacrificed to the brutal egotism of men in this homo-heterosexual triangle (she even goes so far as to spit in Eric's face before leaving her home for the Communist side) and, by demanding that Eric be the one to execute her, she can finally exact her terrible revenge and leave him not only with remorse (*CG,* 151) but, ironically, with the ultimate proof of her love as well—a proof he denies because of his elemental, complete distrust of women: "One is always trapped, somehow, in dealings with women" (*CG,* 151).

His misogyny is not the pose of a man who lacks experience but wishes to appear sophisticated regarding women, nor is it the intellectual conclusion of one too often deceived by them and disabused by love: it is a haughty view of personal relationships that applies to both sexes equally, with the exception of Conrad. In fact, whereas Alexis became a homosexual out of veneration for women, Eric's "vice" is caused much less by his "love for boys" than by his desire for "solitude" (*CG,* 92). This does not mean, however, that he does not find satisfaction, even a certain pleasure, in being loved by Sophie nor that he is so callous and uncaring that, at times, he does not feel amity and affection toward her, going as far as thinking of her as "my Sophie" (*CG,* 70, 82), calling her "Sophie dear" (*CG,* 90), and keeping for sentimental reasons a broken necklace of hers. Too self-contained, too detached to find rewards in human contacts and warmth, he seeks in futile combats the glory of his thirteenth-century ancestors: "Kratovitsy was becoming again what it had been in times supposedly gone by, an outpost of the Teutonic Order, a frontier fortress of the Livonian Brothers of the Sword" (*CG*, 123–24).

It is not for ideological reasons that Eric fights for lost causes, though, since he has a horror of any commitment, political or otherwise, but out of a sense of duty and honor, and also to some degree out of the excitement of action, especially if war can lead to death—a fitting end that is at once an apotheosis and a promotion. His spirit of negation, the brittle personalities of the characters, the closed, stifling atmosphere of Kratovitsy under siege—where they are constantly thrown together and reminded of each other's desires, lies, vexations, evasions, cruelties—as well as their inability to escape from this claustrophobic setting unless it be through ennobling death or an emptiness dragged from continent to continent, from battlefront to battlefront, all this contributes to the ultimate tragedy of the three individuals. And for Eric, now alone and in large measure responsible for previous events, "the drama of [his] existence will be to have lost [Conrad and Sophie] both."[30]

Marguerite Yourcenar is now, at age thirty-six, in complete possession of her literary gifts: she has developed a narrative form whose intricacies she understands well, including the many half-truths found in wholly sincere and objectively lucid accounts;[31] she has evolved themes that are both human and universal; she has become aware of, and interested in, historical research to better convey eternal ideas, along with a way of thinking and feeling about oneself and the world; and, finally, she has developed an acute understanding of man's frailty and, therefore, his unwillingness to compromise with his emotions, often preferring the darker side of love to the blandness of intolerable mediocrity. *Mémoires d'Hadrien,* Yourcenar's next novel and, generally, her first recognized masterpiece, will make full use of all her talents, skills, and knowledge.

Chapter Three
Mémoires d'Hadrien:
Meditations of
a Roman Emperor

Except for a few essays, plays, and poems Marguerite Yourcenar seems, after *Le Coup de grâce*, to be mentally and physically exhausted, a situation she sadly defines as the "lapse into despair of a writer who does not write" (*M, 323*). It was not until the end of 1948 that she resumed her literary pursuits upon receiving from Switzerland a trunk containing, among other things, a few pages of a manuscript beginning "My dear Mark" (*M, 326*): this was to become the beautifully solar *Mémoires d'Hadrien* published in 1951.[1] These imaginary memoirs of the second-century Roman emperor (76–138) were an immediate—and unexpected—success with both the public and the critics. Emile Henriot, for example, calls the novel "exciting," and Robert Kemp praises "a penetrating intelligence which sparkles on every page"; Gérard d'Houville writes that "one feels oneself enriched by a new supply of meditations and of dreams," while André Thérive exclaims, "In seeing the mastery of the author, Flaubert would have roared with admiration!"[2] No less full of enthusiasm, the German novelist Thomas Mann writes glowingly to Claire Goll: "Marguerite Yourcenar . . . has composed the memoirs of Emperor Hadrian with an almost maddening fictional authenticity that is based, by the by, on tremendously solid scholarship. Do you know the book? It is the finest that has come my way in a long time"; and to Karl Kerényi: "Yourcenar's *Memoirs of Hadrian* [is] an erudite artistic composition that has delighted me more than anything else for a long time."[3] The book received the Fémina-Vacaresco Prize[4] and the Grand Novel Prize from the French Academy and was widely translated and read.

The novel is divided into six parts, each having a Latin title taken either from Hadrian's poetry, philosophical ideas, or coins minted during his reign. Each title describes, and each part is devoted to, different phases of the emperor's life, and both correspond to the development not only of his power but also of his personality. For this dual development, Yourcenar traces a slowly rising curve with its apex reached at the time of Hadrian's greatest happiness, the result of his passionate love and extraordinary successes; this euphoria is then followed by an immediately downward slope at the bottom of which the emperor is overcome with doubt and despair; however, in spite of this depression, he courageously embarks on a new beginning: "There is still much to be done" (*M,* 283).[5] The work is addressed to Marcus Aurelius (legally Hadrian's grandson through adoption) in the form of a letter, which allows for the use of the autobiographical "I" favored by Yourcenar as being closest to the human voice. Knowing that his death is fast approaching, Hadrian sets down in the most truthful manner possible, even at the risk of shocking or of not being understood, the important personal and public events of his sixty-odd years, along with his meditations on politics, the arts, and the world. The first part describes the progress of his illness and his renunciation of many activities as his "animula vagula blandula," his "little soul, gentle and drifting" (*M,* 295), is ready to leave his body: "Like the traveler . . . who . . . little by little makes out the shore, I begin to discern the profile of my death" (*M,* 5). Since he wants above all to understand himself, he will rely on the three means at his disposal, that is, books, the observation of others, and, finally, himself, although none gives a complete and undistorted reflection of human existence and psyche.

The second part, titled "Varius multiplex multiformis," shows the variety and complexity of his character. He starts his life story normally enough, in his childhood, when his grandfather, something of a sorcerer, had predicted to the eleven-year-old boy his eventual mastery of the world. After his father's death, Hadrian goes to Rome (he was born in Italica, Spain) and there finishes his schooling. Instead of finding drudgery in his studies, he sees the beauty of philosophy, of grammar (a "mixture of logical rule and arbitrary usage" [*M,* 34]), of rhetoric and poetry, and their useful applicability to human affairs. It is also in Rome that he learns Greek and thus is opened to another world and an almost perfect mode of thinking and being: "Almost everything that men have said best has been said in Greek" (*M,* 35). After returning from a sojourn in Greece, he slowly climbs the ladder of the judicial and military hierarchy, always learning from each situation, from even the most mediocre, the most menial tasks and duties, the reason why and the manner in which man acts and behaves as he does, as well as developing his own commanding and governing style. The diversity of his aptitudes, his intuitive touch during difficult negotiations, his skill on the battlefield, his ruthless taming of rebellious peoples, his personal self-discipline, his interest in barbarian cultures and religions, all of these things bring him to the attention of his cousin, the Emperor Trajan. Yet Trajan is grudge-bearing and indecisive and waits literally (and for the reader, suspensefully) until his dying breath to adopt Hadrian and thereby make him, at forty, the new ruler of the Mediterranean world. That this testament may have been a forgery, committed by Hadrian's friends, especially his good genie Plotina, Trajan's wife, with whom he entertained an "amorous friendship,"[6] does not cause Hadrian any conscience pangs, for he could have endorsed Machiavelli's axiom: "It must be admitted that the end, in this case, was of more concern to me than the means; the essential is that the man invested with power should have proved thereafter that he deserved to wield it" (*M,* 91). His protean *disponibilité* is the result of a desire to comprehend and put everything in a more just light. His is the honest scruple of a man who supremely believes in life and, therefore, in change and movement; he is not a dilettantish Jack-of-all-trades but rather is affected by and open to all situations and human possibilities and always ready to react.

The title "Tellus stabilita," the stabilized earth, expresses well the theme of the third part. Now emperor, Hadrian will seek to establish or maintain the Roman order in the world by intelligent compromises, commercial treaties, and nonaggression pacts, by all-out war and negotiated peace: "Peace was my aim, but not at all my idol . . . I accepted war as a means toward peace where negotiations proved useless in the manner of a physician who decides to cauterize only after having tried simples" (*M,* 97). This section also presents his accomplishments in numerous arenas: public conduct, commerce, laws, slavery, women's status, land reform, peacetime armies, gladiatorial fights, urban planning—all the ideas of an enlightened prince who knows how to keep in equilibrium the conflicting elements of his far-flung rule. After his initiation into the Eleusinian mysteries and his night spent in the Syrian desert he comprehends man's cyclical passing and return and ultimately his own "conscious experience of immortality" (*M,* 149).

In the fourth part, the emperor relates the idyllic years he spent with a Bithynian boy named Antinous.[7] His passion for "this graceful hound, avid both for caresses and commands" (M, 155) finds its origins in the youth's naive innocence as well as in his Greco-Asian beauty and accented speech. "Saeculum aureum," the golden age, is truly that for Hadrian, since it represents the period when his life reaches its apogee; it is a moment when nothing seems impossible, when all is easy. Totally happy, perhaps for the first time, the emperor embarks upon grandiose projects which dot the Greek landscape, and instills in the populace a renewed vitality; he participates fully in the pursuit of the arts and letters, always in the company of Antinous, who sees in him a god and a master and who is concerned with the notion of sacrifice and suicide. "Little by little the light changed" (M, 171), as Hadrian begins to feel constricted in this relationship and seeks in a series of unbridled debauches the freedom from love's too heavy weight, fulfilling a cruel need to vilify and deride the love object the better to leave him. It is no wonder that in the Scamander River plains the highly virile Hadrian visits Achilles' grave whereas the excessively sensitive Antinous prays at Patroclus'. Bloody initiations, occult practices, mediumistic experiments follow one another and lead finally to Antinous' ritual suicide. In the complacent humility of his act the ephebus finds a secret satisfaction and perhaps a hidden pride: through his own death, he hoped to prolong Hadrian's life by having the remainder of his earthly years added to the emperor's. After a long period of despair, Hadrian concludes that he has no "right to detract from the extraordinary masterpiece" which Antinous' departure was and that he must "leave to the boy the credit for his own death" (M, 172–73); unlike Alexander the Great, who destroyed so much when Hephaestion suddenly died, Hadrian creates an almost megalomaniac cult of Antinous by building cities, temples, statues in his favorite's memory. He falls into long lapses of disabused melancholy which makes him notice how quickly others forget their dead and how his own pain is an insulting reminder to them of their own short-lived grief.[8]

In the next part, called "Disciplina Augusta," the august but humane discipline, Hadrian contemplates life and things from a different point of view. Following the terrible ordeal of Antinous' suicide came a time for Hadrian to stop, to think, to read. No longer charmed by easy pleasures, his mind turns to thoughts of immortality. While he has always known that bridges and roads increase by centuries the life of a civilization and that carving his Greek name on the colossus of Memnon may weather the passing of time, he now understands that to avoid Ozymandias' fate he must rely on the immortality granted only by books. He builds libraries ("Dispensary to the Soul" [*M, 228*]) and universities, sponsors vast literary projects, revises his poetry, rereads historians and poets: "The immortality which [the writer] was wont to promise to that youth . . . was more than an empty assurance, since their two memories have come down to me through a space of more than six centuries" (*M, 218*). He is also at work on the construction of his mausoleum and his villa at Tibur (Tivoli)—both the example and model of order and the epitome of the Greek world with its Poecile, Academy, and Prytaneum—interrupted, however, by fits of exasperation, impatience, anger, during one of which he accidentally blinds his secretary: "I had not wished to injure the wretch. But I had not desired, either, that a boy who loved me should die in his twentieth year" (*M, 232–33*).

In Judaea, a revolt led by Simon Bar-Kochba has turned into a full-fledged war that forces the emperor to put on again his military armor and join the front line. After four years of fighting and countless lives lost he is able to brutally crush the last resistance, recognizing nonetheless that this war remains one of his worst failures: "I had not known how to find words which would have prevented, or at least retarded, this outburst of fury in a nation; I had not known in time how to be either supple enough or sufficiently firm" (*M, 239*). In fact, despite his tolerance of pagan customs and practices, he is unwilling to accept either the Christian or the Jewish religions, whose representatives he qualifies (not without evident bad faith) as narrow-minded, ignorant, inflexible, fanatical, sectarian, and blinded. He sees in their doctrines ideas that not only run against human nature but might ultimately sap the very foundations of the state, because they are turned toward Heaven and not toward the Eternal City. Like any colonialist, Hadrian is confronted with the unsettling discovery that not all countries regard the civilizing influences of Greece and Rome as necessary or at least useful: "I offered this despised people a place among the others in the Roman community," he bitterly exclaims (*M, 191*); he is further astonished to realize that there exist other ways of living and other relationships with God which reject his pluralistic conception of the perfect society in particular and his world view in general, even if this refusal means annihilation and dispersal. In punishment, "Judaea was struck from the map and took the name of Palestine by my order" (*M,* 249).

It is also during this Middle Eastern campaign that he suffered his first heart seizure, and the rapid deterioration of his health (he probably had cardiac edema) renders the selection of his successor all the more pressing since he wishes to avoid the contentious troubles that accompanied his own accession to the throne. After the emperor has examined the careers of several potential nominees, he adopts Lucius Ceionius (Aelius Caesar), who had been an early lover. When Lucius dies of tuberculosis, Hadrian quickly adopts Antoninus, an excellent administrator and a virtuous senator, with the added order that he, in turn, take Marcus Aurelius as his adopted son: "My imperial heritage was safe in the hands of the devoted Antoninus and the grave Marcus Aurelius. . . . All that was not too badly arranged" (*M,* 271).

Death, or rather a meditation on death, is the subject of the last part, entitled "Patientia." If at first Hadrian considers suicide as an appropriate method of overcoming the disgust of living, he concludes that such an act would in his case show ingratitude to his friends, along with uncustomary cowardice: "The time of impatience has passed; . . . despair would be in as bad taste as hope itself. I have ceased to hurry my death" (*M,* 283). The ghosts of those he loved are not far from him, dreams and presages now portend the approach of death, his friends' sorrow confirms their faithful love, even the disillusion of seeing that Rome is not especially favored by the gods and to a large extent may be on her downward slide cannot destroy the appeased calm of his final days: "Let us try . . . to enter death with open eyes" (*M,* 295).

Quoting Flaubert's "unforgettable sentence," "Just when the gods had ceased to be, and the Christ had not yet come, there was a unique moment in history, between Cicero and Marcus Aurelius, when man stood alone" (*M,* 319–20), Yourcenar wants to portray a great historical personage who, thanks to his broad humanist culture and inquiring intelligence, was able to dominate without illusions his life and times with as much objectivity and lucidity as possible. Hadrian is at once an aesthete, an art lover, a poet, an indefatigable traveler, a general, an economist, a master builder, a political scientist who was the first to think of creating "a kind of federal empire in which every region of the world would have its part,"[9] in other words, he is a man deeply interested in everything who learned very early "to value things above words, to mistrust mere formulas, and to observe rather than to judge" (*M,* 37).

Armed with this method he can look at man, his institutions, and the world and, especially, help reform them because he sees his "different professions" (*M,* 123) as continuing the work of the great Greek and Roman innovators and rulers and also, at the end of his life, as preventing the empire from crumbling and perhaps from falling apart altogether. When Hadrian came to power in 117 A.D., the empire was threatened on all sides and on the verge of economic collapse with the contributing classes exhausted following the ten years of useless wars conducted by Trajan: "The dying emperor would cover himself with glory, and we who must go on living would have to resolve all the problems and remedy all the evils" (*M,* 80). Yourcenar's book is more than the autobiography of Emperor Hadrian, however; it can further be considered a manual for princes in which is explained how human knowledge and consciousness and imperial knowledge and consciousness can be united in order to govern better, and what the necessary elements are to make a good prince. In his all-encompassing outlook on the world in which he lives, Hadrian is a kind of unique "Everyman," a representative of the people, without demagoguery, who at the same time stands apart from them, thus allowing his rare genius full play in all areas of human endeavor. In a master stroke after becoming emperor, Hadrian immediately returned some of the conquered lands (Assyria, Mesopotamia, Armenia) since he felt that Rome's hegemony was not enforceable. More open to compromise than his predecessor, he is willing to recognize too, as Janet Whatley has well indicated, that territorial expansion is no longer advisable and that a policy of conquest had actually become harmful;[10] this change of direction was concretely put into effect with the erection of a wall to separate England from Scotland.

After his accession to the purple Hadrian revitalized commerce and industry by the judicious decrease of taxes and duties; to foster the free trade of goods (including as an additional benefit the exportation of Roman ideas and customs) he built or widened harbors and encouraged the improvement of the merchant marine; he took pride in creating fishermen's cooperatives; he sought the experienced advice and information of bankers and merchants; he fought against middlemen and monopolistic cartels; he prevented the chaotic price surges of common staples; and, above all, he wanted to have again a strong currency backed with accurate and real reserves in goods and services ("it behooves us to give [our gold coins] solid weight and true value in terms of commodities"), because he knew such monetary strength to symbolize "Rome's eternity" (M, 117). While the emperor shows in his economic programs the solid common sense of an Adam Smith, he turns to writers like Plato for his political theories, but always adapts them to current causes and circumstances in order to constantly improve his subjects' condition. He is practical and pragmatic enough that, in appreciating the beauty of such treatises as *The Republic,* he has taken their daring views and gone further by actually implementing many of them both in the restructuring of a state which would thus become less oppressive in its heavy-handedness and more responsive to man's needs while less intrusive in his daily life, and in codifying better, because simpler, laws (his Perpetual Edict was the basis for the Justinian Code): "I proposed as my aim a prudent avoidance of superfluous decrees, and the firm promulgation, instead, of a small group of well-weighted decisions" (M, 113) which by their force of precedent could last forever.

His generous nature leads him to improve the status of slaves through proper regulation, although he suspects that fundamentally slavery will never be abolished since other, more insidious forms of enslavement will simply take its place under different appellations and be just as inhuman as slavery in fact. In addition, he works to modify the ambiguous legal condition of women who "are at one and the same time subjugated and protected, weak and powerful, too much despised and too much respected" (M, 116); yet, despite his otherwise forward-looking liberalism, he remains a man of his century by his lack of understanding for women as individual and equal human beings, assserting that in general they are what they wish to be, that they also resist change lest it cause them unpredictable harm, and that they content themselves with running households and businesses at which they seem adept and from which they draw unlimited power. Therefore, he will restrict himself to passing laws increasing women's rights to manage their own fortunes, to inherit, to make bequests, and, given marriage's great importance in their eyes, not to marry against their will. (If this law had been in effect when *he* married Sabina, she may have been less unhappy, less bitter and shrewish.)

This legal fine-tuning underscores Hadrian's reluctance to completely overhaul customs which themselves result from age-old experience and conclusions in which, obviously, nature played a crucial part: his entire conception of women is summarized by a very Freudian "biology is destiny." Even in their mental processes women think as women, whereas thinking man "belongs to his species rather than to his sex" and eventually transcends the human as well (*M,* 63). Love, too, is different for women since it hardly ever causes terrifying and exalting upheavals in their hearts. What is for Hadrian an astonishing miracle is degraded by women to the rank of an expensive bauble or some new makeup, the better to reinforce the theatrical staginess of their oaths, their quarrels, their remorses. Men are evidently often taken in by the exterior—and artificial—charms of these goddesses, "attach[ing] themselves at least as much to the temple and to the accessories of the cult . . ., delight[ing] in the red fingernails and in the] perfumes rubbed on the skin, and in the thousand devices which enhance that beauty and sometimes fabricate it entirely" (*M,* 62). Never far from women's minds are worries about children, money, clothes; and Hadrian's mistresses always give him the impression that once they have returned to their homes they will resume their petty preoccupations. On the other hand, Hadrian gives himself totally and unconstrainedly to love, which he equates to a religious initiation in which "sacred" and "secret" are finally merged. Because love opens a new universe of physical and emotional sensations, the loved one acquires a forceful presence in his life, going as far as to "unsettle the soul" (*M,* 12) and reason. This abandonment of logic and lucidity, this wonderful "sunstroke of love" (*Y,* 74), points out Hadrian's quest for happiness, almost in a desperate attempt to catch up with life. There was always, of course, pleasure in doing his work well, in spreading civilization to the far reaches of the globe, but it was not until his encounter with Antinous at forty-seven that the "golden age" began and his happiness was highest: "Someone wiser than I might well have remained happy till his death" (*M,* 164). After the Bithynian killed himself, Hadrian knew that he had lost more than he possessed. It is this knowledge and the nostalgic memory of his attachment which, combined with his own guilt feelings, confer on his passion an unreal luster, due in large part to the freeze-frame quality of the young man's suicide and its indelible impression on Hadrian, since death has removed this divine being from future human imperfections and deteriorations. In retrospect, however, his "sacrifice will have enriched not my life but my death" (M, 290) by helping the emperor to bear with "patience" the attacks of his malady and to accept himself with serenity.

He adapts the same eclectic ideas to his pursuits of the arts. He not only tried his hand at painting still lifes and writing poetry (oftentimes resenting—humanly enough—his critics' acerbic comments) or at playing ancient Attic melodies on his long flute, but he also enjoyed the company of learned and cultivated men and encouraged their works in all genres, especially in architecture and sculpture. Whether all these artists and writers were of the first order or not matters little, for all that really counts is that they "were more or less caught up in the dream" (M, 133), adding the fruits of their labors to the enlightening radiance brought by the Roman Peace. Moreover, raised in the tradition of a sound mind in a sound body, Hadrian extols the merits of vigorous activities, from horseback riding to wrestling to hunting. To engage in exercise, as Jacques Vier suggests, is to inhale the sky and to feel underfoot the wondrous powers of the earth;[11] for Hadrian, these same incredible powers are manifest in even the simple act of, for example, eating a peach—an experience that links together two products, the man and the fruit, of this selfsame earth. In sports and in battle the body is viewed as a good servant, a faithful companion, a sure friend who deserves respect and obedience ("all my life long I have trusted in the wisdom of my body" [M, 283]) and finally, by its being the soul's host, it is the necessary co-requisite of an essence as well.

His attitude toward his job and position is exemplified by his statement, "We emperors are not Caesars; we are functionaries of the State" (M, 120–21), and finds its explanation in his regard for all the people in his care. Although fully cognizant of their defects, he knows very well that he is like them and, therefore, he cannot despise them, otherwise "I should have no right, and no reason, to try to govern" them (M, 41). All his life he has wanted to better their lot by the wise application of three basic concepts—humanity, happiness, and liberty—tempered by discipline and patience, and he vehemently refuses to believe that the masses are unworthy of such lofty intentions simply because it may end in their becoming somehow corrupt and complacent, as if there would not always be other reasons for suffering and misery, including the large disparity between the rich and the poor. On the contrary, by relying on their virtues and self-esteem rather than complaining about their short-comings, Hadrian believed that they would for the most part respond positively to kindness, probity, and courage; even if they did not, to act differently would only bring rebellion and perhaps an end to the state itself: "All nations who have perished up to this time have done so for lack of generosity" (*M,* 114).

Acknowledging that his role is to impose Greek thought in all human endeavors, the emperor seeks to create a universe of perfect harmony and beauty, where "the might and the majesty of the Roman Peace should extend to all" (*M,* 134). Indeed, violence and war represent for him the greatest evils, and peace and liberty the requirements necessary for civilization's gentle suasion. Further-more, the collaboration of intelligence and work in such a beneficial environment will bring happiness to all. Not surprisingly, Hadrian was able to accomplish most of his objectives thanks not only to his talents and skills, to his keen appreciation of his and Rome's destiny, the *"quid divinum"* shared by the protagonists in *Denier du rêve* (*O,* 162), but also to the vastness of his views, the conduct and the ethic "of a man placed at the top of the human pyramid, but never duped, never intoxicated, never seized by vertigo."[12] Accord-ingly, honorific titles are accepted either with a certain irony ("my duties forced me to serve as the incarnation of . . . Providence for one part of mankind" [*M,* 145]) or as actually merited. His is the exemplary career of an upper-echelon civil servant whose many con-tributions to the empire and to the welfare of its populations have been demonstrated. There is, however, still another aspect of his character that makes Hadrian a fascinating personality. A triple figure, he belongs to the past, he is a pragmatist of and for his time, and he possesses an acute sense of the future.

First, he sees himself as the continuator of the twelve Caesars, happy that he does not have to create out of chaotic beginnings a viable political system, and, naturally, the Greek heritage is evident everywhere in his thoughts and deeds. Hadrian would only concur with the remarks Yourcenar made in a 1980 interview: "To study ancient civilizations is to get a complete image of how society develops, succeeds, and fades. . . . We get a blueprint of . . . what mankind can and cannot do under different circumstances."[13] Aware of his historical and intellectual origins, he can rebuild the empire and leave his mark on it by using consistently the lessons of the past, yet without being its slave: "I shall have been the first,

perhaps, to subordinate all my actions to this 'spirit of the times,'
to make of it something other than the inflated dream of a philosopher, or the slightly vague aspirings of some good prince" (*M,*
111). Finally, his observations concerning the future events of the
world, while seeming altogether too prescient, are quite plausible
educated guesses, provided, Yourcenar cautions, "such prognostics
remain vague and general" (*M,* 332). Hadrian foresees a strong
Great Britain, a power shift away from the Mediterranean countries
to those of the Atlantic, the circumnavigation of the globe, and the
discovery of China and its wonders; he foresees also a glorious and
lasting monument to Rome, in that every nation, every town will
be regulated in one form or another by its wise experience. Even if
the bishop of Christ succeeds in replacing the pagan high priest,
he too "will have become in his turn one of the universal figures of
authority. He . . . will differ from rulers like us less than one
might suppose" (*M,* 294). Perhaps Hadrian's work will become
useless, but in having delayed the invasions of the hordes he has
helped for a time the empire's survival, and in the end these bar-
barians also will be Romanized and will acquire that certain way of
looking at and thinking of the world. This, then, is how Rome
will remain eternal in the emperor's eyes; the rest, of course, is left
to the gods.

   Memoirs of Hadrian has often been referred to as an historical
novel.[14] Yourcenar's book, however, is not really an historical novel
according to the general criteria of the genre, since it rejects the
facile use of paraphernalia, local color, period dress, and quaint
customs—what Yourcenar calls "a kind of costume ball 'in
technicolor' "[15]—prevalent in such works as Honoré de Balzac's *The
Duchess of Langeais,* Alexandre Dumas's *The Three Musketeers,* or Gustave Flaubert's *Salammbô.* At the same time, *Memoirs of Hadrian* is
not disguised either as a history textbook which "under the very
thin pretext of a filiform adventure [teaches] us all one can know
about the manner in which people of a certain period used to eat,
to dress, to take walks, etc."[16] It is actually a mix of the two types,
for, on the one hand, in Aristotle's phrase, "it relates what has
happened" as well as shows extensive scholarly research on the second-century emperor, complemented by the author's frequent trips
to Rome and to the Villa Adriana in Tibur and by an erudite reliance
on art and artifacts of and about the Hadrianic era—an era in which
Yourcenar saturated herself with the details of whatever she was

investigating until her mind selected as salient and useful whatever answered her psychological or intellectual needs.[17] On the other hand, the *Mémoires* deals with the fictional and the psychoanalytical, which are the realm of literature.

Although she does not go so far as to follow T. S. Eliot's advice, given in his famous 1919 essay on "Tradition and the Individual Talent," to transform the past in the light of the present conditions, Yourcenar does show that the Roman period of Hadrian's rule is very close to ours by portraying a highly sophisticated, complex, and skeptical emperor who reveals through the clear presentation of a temporal succession of events all the aspects of his political and emotional life. In this fashion, the author has truly penetrated deep into the heart and mind of her character. Even so, the emperor observes in his letter to Marcus Aurelius that the most sincere of books always distort the truth and lie, that "the less adroit, for lack of words and phrases wherein they can enclose life, retain of it but a flat and feeble likeness," and that historical discourse itself renders the sequence of causes and effects and of motivations and reactions "much too exact and clear to have been ever entirely true . . ." (*M*, 22).[18] This distrust of history is, of course, well-founded if all that it is is a fixation or an arbitrary intellectualization of life. But for both Yourcenar and Hadrian it in fact represents at once a search for lost time in the Proustian sense of re-creating past and self ("searching out the reasons of its existence, its starting point, and its source" [*M*, 26]) and an attempt at understanding man by studying one's own nature, a kind of fictionalized version of Montaigne's *Essais* which would neither be an "apologia pro sua vita," necessarily defensive and self-serving, nor a totally objective presentation of historical reality and human truth. The Emperor Hadrian, who characterizes himself partly through accounts of his actions, more often through perspicacious analyses of his thoughts and feelings, fits very well with the known facts and is so subtly portrayed that even his persona seems to explain the facts. With a talent which gives the novelist precedence over the historian and the moralist and philosopher precedence over the novelist, Yourcenar resuscitates a conception of man and life at the end of a great civilization. This is how this insightful projection of imagined memoirs refutes Paul Valéry's attack on history as being "the most dangerous product."[19] Instead, Yourcenar asserts that history might be one of the most valuable constructs our intelligence has ever devised since, as Robert

Champigny has pointed out, "the novelistic field is closed, whereas the historical field is open: in the case of the novel, the contained events are uncorrectable and complete; in the case of history, new information can always bring extensions and modifications."[20]

As Yourcenar wrote in her notebooks appended to *Memoirs of Hadrian,* life is schematized by "what a man believed himself to be and what he wished to be, plus . . . what he actually was" (*M,* 341); it seems evident, therefore, that no one can be completely faithful to the historical truth and that at times the emperor was probably lying, since one is always tempted to be lenient with oneself, or that at least he was refusing to ask the hard questions (for instance, after Trajan's death) in order to attain the full and complete truth. Furthermore, Hadrian deviates from the recorded truth because Yourcenar is not presenting the picture of an epoch or dealing with an emperor in time, but with an emperor *out of time* and with the collective sensibility or consciousness that has taken this particular and very special Roman for its spokesman.[21]

In one of her essays, Yourcenar notes that the present by its nature enters from the very first the category of the historical account and that it has no privileged place in the course of the centuries.[22] According to A. A. Mendilow, while historical fiction rarely succeeds in giving the illusion of presentness and immediacy due to the distance existing between historical time and narrative time,[23] *Memoirs of Hadrian* is able to incorporate the historical instant into a cosmic idea of eternity and to telescope the antinomy of the present's omnipresence and of the eternal recurrence by using what Jean Blot has defined as the "double past," that is, the merging of the "historical" and "narrative" pasts[24] as the emperor "begin[s] to discern [eighteen centuries ago] the profile of my death" (*M,* 5). Yourcenar further remarked during a radio interview that "this kind of look . . . lets us embrace time all at once, time in which the character has lived, and also ours."[25]

The conflict between Hadrian's individual will and the inscrutable world will allows for a critical awareness of a long range of vision by equating the given period to the past and future, sometimes explicitly, always implicitly. This makes the ancient period both the setting and the choral comment. Indeed, an important device of historical fiction is to have characters make anticipations or predictions (what Gérard Genette calls "temporal prolepses")[26] about the future state of the world. Although such "prophetic insights"

(M, 332) assert a new historical reality and break the contemporary present's illusion, they also develop it into an historical continuum, emphasizing that these intuitions are but a moment in man's fantastic adventure. According to Avrom Fleishman, this in fact is the aesthetic function of the novelist-historian: "To lift the contemplation of the past above both the present and the past, to see it in its universal character, freed of the urgency of historical engagement. The reflection from the present to the past is completed when the historical novelist reaches not the present from which he began but the constants of human experience in history—however these may appear to him in his time and place."[27]

In order to re-create Hadrian's modes of living and being as well as his conflict between public and private values, Yourcenar chose a style that "is very close to history's since the dying Hadrian is to a large degree his own historian, his own Plutarch. . . . He reconstructs his past in a certain manner, insisting on what still matters to him, disdaining the rest, as we all do."[28] This is why both time and space can easily be shortened or bridged: "Fifteen years with the armies have lasted less long than a single morning at Athens. . . . Planes in space overlap likewise" (M, 25–26); and in her "Reflections" Yourcenar adds "that one can contract the distance between centuries at will" (M, 330), a technique that quite naturally echoes Marcel Proust's own in depicting the fleeting quality of Time: "To render its fleetingness sensitive, novelists are required, through the frenzied acceleration of the tickings of the pendulum, to get the reader to cross ten, twenty, thirty years in two minutes."[29]

The style of *Mémoires* is not that of the interior monologue in the usual meaning of the word, but what has been described as the interior discourse, in which the emperor speaks in the first person because, as Yourcenar explains, "I hoped, in making him speak himself, to arrive at the point where man expresses himself in terms of his own life, his own destiny, instead of making him go through our own opinions and our own comments."[30]

From the point of view of historical fiction *Memoirs of Hadrian* has few parallels. The nearest approach to what Yourcenar has accomplished might be found in Thornton Wilder's *The Ides of March* and to a lesser extent in Walter Pater's *Marius the Epicurean*, Robert Graves's *I, Claudius*, or Hermann Broch's *The Death of Vergil*. Yourcenar differs from writers of historical novels in her willingness to take the existential risk through the experience of her Roman hero. She can emphasize today's need for "intelligence, simplicity, goodness, justice." Indeed, it is through her sovereign's life that she shows "her sadness and concern in view of the state of the world,"[31] thereby rejoining Arnold Toynbee's own insight regarding the contemporaneity of the present and the past: "Whatever chronology might say, Thucydides' world and my world have now proved to be philosophically contemporary. . . . This vision . . . of the philosophical contemporaneity of all civilizations was fortified by being seen against a background provided by some of the discoveries of our modern . . . physical science."[32]

The success of this novel, "strong and grave, as one seldom finds,"[33] confirmed for Yourcenar that her historical method was sound and that through the retelling of the life of the "deified August Hadrian" (M, 296) she had in fact exposed universal truths and explored archetypes that have their origins in Western culture. She has demonstrated that her Roman emperor not only incarnates the serene *patientia romana* of "a man who was *almost* wise" (M, 327) but represents also the fears and aspirations of thinking readers who find in this reconstruction of the past "the accomplishment in its plenitude of a statesman's destiny, and in sum of a human being . . ." (Y, 159). The intense style, the solid though unpedantic erudition, the psychological characterizations and understanding, the philosophical themes and metaphysical ideas of *L'Oeuvre au noir* will draw considerably upon and benefit from Yourcenar's experience and from the magnificent achievement of *Mémoires d'Hadrien*.

Chapter Four
L'Oeuvre au noir:
A New Alchemy

As in previous works, in this novel, Marguerite Yourcenar once again re-creates an era with its particular modes of thinking and being. Her use of an alchemical formula for the French title, *l'oeuvre au noir,* conveys the essential themes. The *opus nigrum,* the work in black, describes in alchemical treatises the "attempt at dissolution and calcination of forms which is the first but most difficult part of the Great Work."[1] The English translation takes its name from the title of one of the book's crucial chapters, "The Abyss," as well as from the *abyssus* necessary, according to Paracelsus, to gain immortality.[2]

As Yourcenar mentions in her appended note, the novel first appeared in 1934 in the form of a short story, "D'après Dürer" (In the manner of Dürer), published with two other stories as *La Mort conduit l'attelage* (Death drives the team) (*A,* 359–60). Certain protagonists, Zeno, the hero, and his cousin, Henri-Maximilien, are already present with their ideas and personalities well delineated, one a military adventurer off to join Francis I's army, the other "an adventurer of knowledge."[3] The same genealogy exists in both books, the same questionings of social, religious, and philosophical concepts and principles, the future soldier asking "Why?," and the young philosopher, "Why not?" (*Mo,* 66–67). Present in both narratives are Zeno's wanderings across Europe and the Mediterranean basin as he tries to escape from the church authorities for writings considered heretical, as well as the panoramic fresco of the sixteenth century and the early years of the Reformation, including illuminated religious movements and sects.

L'Oeuvre au noir (1968) is divided into three parts, the first two parts echoing each other ("Wandering Life" and "Immobile Life") and the third ("The Prison") describing at once the site of Zeno's last two months and acting as a metaphor for his body and the world. The action takes place between 1510 and 1569 in Catholic Europe, especially in the Belgian city of Bruges.

On the road leading out of Bruges, having abandoned his formal university studies, Zeno is on his way to Santiago de Compostela to meet the prior of the Jacobites of León, an ardent practitioner of alchemy, to see the world ("Who would be so besotted as to die without having made at least the round of this, his prison?" [A, 11]), and to learn about himself. He is accompanied part of the way by Henri-Maximilien Ligre, his cousin, who wants to enlist in the French army and perhaps win honor and glory on some Italian battlefield. In a series of flashbacks, the former's background and character are revealed and explained.

Zeno, whose name is associated with the Greek negator of movement, as well as with "zero" and "no," was born in Bruges on 24 February 1510 (A, 267),[4] the illegitimate child of Messer Alberico de' Numi, a young Italian prelate who became cardinal at thirty, and of Hilzonde Ligre, the daughter of an important Flemish family. Hilzonde's brother, Henri-Juste, is the head of this wealthy and powerful family of textile manufacturers and bankers, associated with the Fuggers of Cologne. When Alberico is accidentally killed after a Roman orgy, Hilzonde marries Simon Adriansen, a good and pious Anabaptist, who brings her a certain serenity and a renewed self-esteem. Zeno is raised in the house of his uncle, Henri-Juste, with the expectation that he will enter the church either as a cleric or a university theologian, since he shows from very early on his "mania for learning" (A, 23), particularly for philosophical problems and the sciences. Under the tutoring of Canon Bartholommé Campanus, he learns Greek, Latin, the natural sciences, and alchemy; if at first he marvels at his discoveries he quickly realizes like Hadrian before him "that books lie and speak folly, just as men do" (A, 24). A true *homo universalis* of the Renaissance, Zeno invents a weaving machine, discusses the atoms of Epicurus and the proofs demonstrating God's existence, refuses a priori the authority of Plato, Aristotle, and Plutarch, and dares to go beyond the timorous lessons of his Louvain University professors. He is similarly interested in geology and botany, in medicine and surgery, in astronomy and metallurgy, but his pursuits and his dark beauty frighten his uncle. Ultimately disgusted by his compatriots' stupidity and fear, Zeno entrusts his notebooks to his best friend, Jean Myers, and leaves for Spain.

Public opinion would have it that he performed human dissections in Paris, that he studied medicine in Montpellier, that he engaged in horrible blood transfusions in Catalonia, that he discovered the Greek fire which helped the Turks destroy the Spanish fleet at Algiers, that he practiced medicine in Hungary but refused to become the doge's personal physician, that in Basel he miraculously healed those stricken with black plague. Some of these rumored activities, as he himself will later confide to his cousin, were indeed true, others completely fabricated, occasionally even by himself, while a few were not even known: travels to Damascus, Constantinople, Pera, Lyons where he spoke with Lorenzaccio de' Medici. In addition, he published his findings on the physiology of the heart and on arteries and blood circulation.

In the meantime, his mother, under the gentle influence of her husband, Simon Adriansen, turns toward the Reformed faith which endorses a more equitable distribution of riches, secular and divine. When Simon proposes to her that they both depart within fourteen days for Münster, the City of God founded by Jan Matthyjs and Hans Bockhold, the new king and messiah, she immediately replies, "My husband, the fortnight is already passed" (*A,* 64).[5] There, under siege by Catholic forces, the Just, the Saints, the Good, the Pure, as they are alternately called, destroy Catholic idols and images and give in to a series of frenetic activities caused as much by hunger as by unbridled ecstasy. As a result, Hilzonde becomes one of Hans's eighteen wives after he has her "go into the backroom, where he lift[s] her robes to show the young Prophets how white and pure is the naked Church" (*A,* 70). When the bishop's troops invade the city, they execute most of the faithful, and Hilzonde is beheaded. Simon Adriansen, who had been absent during the siege, dies of heart failure and old age shortly thereafter, and their daughter, Martha, is then sent to live with the Fuggers (Adriansen's sister is married to Martin Fugger). In Cologne, behind appearances of Roman Catholic orthodoxy, the young girl embraces wholeheartedly the antipopish tenets of Calvinism in which she sees "a faith cleansed of all error, exempt of all weakness, strict in its liberty, in short, rebellion transformed into law" (*A,* 90). The terrible plague of 1549 kills many inhabitants of the Rhineland, including several in the Fugger household. Zeno, unable to save the Fuggers' daughter, Bénédicte, learns during a conversation with his half-sister Martha that his mother and her husband have died in Münster. Martha is

therefore heiress to the Fugger fortune and soon after marries her
first cousin, Philibert Ligre, thereby merging two vast financial
empires.

When Henri-Maximilien and Zeno meet again, this time in Innsbruck, they recount to one another all their previous activities. One,
in search of elusive knowledge, has traveled extensively; the other
has, as hoped, distinguished himself in war and has been praised
by Blaise de Monluc, but is far from the happiness he had expected
from it. Their conversation also reveals the depth and daring of
Zeno's thought and the philosophical distance covered between his
departure from Bruges and now. Feeling that he is again under
suspicion, however, he flees just in time to avoid arrest by the
Inquisition, and Henri-Maximilien, too, rushes to regain Italy where
he dies outside Siena, pages of his manuscript, "Blazon of Woman's
Body," flying in the February wind. Zeno finds a refuge in Würz-
burg, then in Poland; from there he embarks for Sweden where he
becomes King Gustavus Vasa's physician and the doubting master
astrologer of his son Erik, reminding the young man that "the stars,
though they influence our destinies, do not determine them" (A,
139). Once again, though, the philosopher's life is in danger, and
he runs off to Lübeck and Louvain under the name of a dead German
medical practitioner, Dr. Gott, which he changes to Sébastien Theus,
the better to hide. He then goes off to Paris and is well received
by Ruggieri who introduces him to Queen Catherine de' Medici,
but when he understands that she will do nothing to prevent the
destruction of his latest work, he decides to stop his "wandering
life," returns to Bruges after a thirty-odd-year absence, and shares
the house of his old friend, Jean Myers. When the latter is poisoned
by his own maid who has committed this murder out of love and
animal devotion for Zeno, he immediately turns all Myers's money
over to the Hospice of St. Cosmus, run by the Order of Franciscans,
of which he assumes the medical responsibility, while the maid
Catherine remains a servant in the Myers house, now a home for
the aged.

The prior of the Franciscans, a good and learned man, and Zeno
have daily conversations about religion and questions of faith, as
well as about the deteriorating state of affairs in Flanders, the punishing repression of the patriots by Spanish forces, and the intolerant
tortures and killings of Catholics and Protestants alike. Although
Zeno enjoys these exchanges, he considers them artificial because

he sees the need to dissimulate his true feelings and, in a sense, to reflect in his words his friend's anguish and suffering, when in fact this wave of terror and executions is nothing new to him, so used is he to "un monde à feu et à sang" (*O*, 714; "a world devastated by war" [*A*, 204]). Despite these feelings, he is still willing to heal the assassin of a Spanish officer, who is also a destroyer of religious images, and to ask the prior for money to help this same person escape to Antwerp, regardless of the futility of any action in an absurd universe. (Ironically, instead of joining the rebels, the fellow hires out as a carpenter aboard a slave ship bound for Africa.)

When one of his assistants, a young monk named Cyprien, tells him of his nightly activities as a member of a group of "Angels" who make love to the "Fair One" and her maid "naked as they would be in Paradise" (*A*, 228), a remnant of lustful practices and metaphorical images of forbidden sects thought to have disappeared at the turn of the sixteenth century, Zeno knows that the prudent course of action would be to leave the region, particularly after his protector's death. He chooses, however, not to cross over to England or Zeeland since ultimately escape leads nowhere and he would undoubtedly find in these countries the same lies, superstitions, and compromises, and "perhaps, after all, he might never be disturbed in Bruges" (*A*, 268). Such is not the case, though. After the "Fair One" becomes pregnant and, in desperation and shame, kills her prematurely born infant, she is quickly apprehended and denounces her lover, giving his name and confessing all the sexual doings of the naive band of "Angels." Cyprien is questioned and, to avoid torture for himself, tells everything, adding and inventing as he goes along. Because of the young monk's confession, Zeno is arrested. As in his decision not to leave, the same acceptance of and resignation to fatality are evident here: "One always falls into some kind of trap; so it might as well be that one" and "he astonishe[s] everyone by giving his true name" to the judges (*A*, 285).

While the charges against Zeno for complicity in the debauches of the young monks and girls are quickly dismissed, there remain, of course, the very important crimes of his apparent sympathy for the rebels' cause and of his blasphemous writings which were condemned and burned for their blatant impiety. In all, twenty-four indictments are retained against him. Defending his own case before the tribunal of exception, Zeno argues about physiology, astronomy, and physics, always rejecting unscientific hypotheses and conclusions. In the end, understandably, he is condemned because he instinctively knows that there can exist "no lasting accord . . . between those who seek, ponder, and dissect, and pride themselves on being capable of thinking tomorrow otherwise than they do today, and those who accept the Faith, or declare that they do, and oblige their fellow men to do the same, on pain of death" (A, 317). Seeing the hopelessness of the situation, Zeno's boyhood tutor, Canon Campanus, asks Zeno's half-sister and cousin-brother-in-law to intervene on the accused's behalf, but they find it more expedient to do nothing, now that they have acquired nobiliary status. The old priest has one long conversation with his former pupil during which each sees the wide gulf that separates them; there is, however, a way out for Zeno: to recant, to definitively disown his books and words, to retract them all publicly. He rejects this retraction of his entire existence, not out of courage but out of "some indefinable blind refusal" which comes from his being "already . . . *in aeternum*" (A, 348). Yet, afraid to die at the stake, Zeno chooses the more personal death found in suicide and slashes his tibial vein and the radial artery at his left wrist with a hidden blade. Even then, he studies his own reactions as the blood slowly drains from his body. Thus he dies on 17 February 1569, on the eve of Mardi Gras, one week short of his fifty-ninth birthday.

Again Yourcenar uses solid historical, biographical, and scientific material to provide the "specific reality conditioned by time and place . . ." (A, 361).[6] She explains in her note that her main character owes much to Leonardo da Vinci, Campanella, Paracelsus, Erasmus, Nicolas Flamel, and other seekers of truth of the Renaissance.[7] Yet Zeno is, of course, more than a synthetic amalgam of famous thinkers. Jean Blot sees the hero as an "anti-Hadrian, . . . a fluid, . . . a metal which liquefies, and erupted lava," due more to their opposite temperaments—one Mediterranean and solar, the other Northern and lunar—than to their intellectual concerns, alive in a world "in fusion, gestation, or flux."[8] It is this chaotic life which is the subject of the novel.

Obsessed by the accumulation of knowledge, Zeno is especially fearful of being trapped by bookish authorities or complacent ways of seeing and thinking. Hence, he is a rationalist at a time of religious obscurantism, an agnostic questioning the existence of God ("One who perchance Is" [A, 11]), a skeptic endowed with limited free will who must contribute to his own development, according to the phrase from Pico della Mirandola placed in epigraph at the beginning of part 1: "I have made you neither celestial nor terrestrial, neither mortal nor immortal, so that, like a free and able sculptor and painter of yourself, you may mold yourself wholly in the form of your choice" (*A*, 3). The title of an early chapter, "Les Enfances de Zénon" ("Zeno's Boyhood"), by its very medieval ring, gives the notion of several childhoods devoted to particular endeavors, in which creativity and curiosity are tempered with a highly developed critical sense and in which, too, fire, what Gaston Bachelard defines as "one of the principles of universal explanation,"[9] plays an important role. The baby was born at the light of an open hearth, and later his handsome good looks are heightened by "the dark fire of his eyes" (*A*, 26); he is seen as a frequent companion of fire; his presence is feared like that of "a burning brand in a barn" (*A*, 49) since, as Yourcenar herself qualifies him, he is all "fire and flame" (*Y*, 172), and there is also the fire connected with alchemical experiments. Curiously enough, however, the novel is not concerned with the transmutation of base metals, in or out of an athanor (as a matter of fact, Zeno has none of the tools needed for this occult trade and, in an ironic aside, accuses his Innsbruck landlord of overcharging, thereby making gold from his tenants), but with the quest for knowledge devoid of falsehood, superstition, fear, and ignorance. It is this search for the absolute that distinguishes Zeno from other scientists and makes of him a universal man, lucid in his thinking, unwilling to accept any fanaticism, whether philosophical, scientific, moral, or religious.

In wandering through the world, he realizes that "everything suffers change, both the form of the world and what Nature produces in its motion, each moment of which takes centuries" (*A*, 35), but also that people are everywhere the same, with their allotted share of "ignorance and fear, stupidity and hypocrisy" (*A*, 53). In the first of a series of summing up of experiences since his departure from Bruges, we witness in "A Conversation in Innsbruck" the evolution of Zeno's thought from the young scholar who rejected his uncle's bourgeois universe, a comfortable position in the church or university hierarchy,[10] and a god, born of a virgin, who resuscitates on the third day, to the learned physician who sees the human body as the microcosm "in which is repeated the structure of the Whole" and where the brain is the seat of the soul (*A*, 112). After years of experimentation and study, Zeno has come to the awareness

that the "human machine" (A, 172) itself, like the outside world
it imitates, is an excellent alchemist involved in "the transmutation
of corpses, those of beasts and of plants, into living matter, sepa-
rating the useful from the dross without any help from" it (A, 174)
and is alternately re-created through this ingestion of food and
destroyed by fatigue and old age.

When Zeno calls man "One who Is" (A, 122), using the formula
and capital letters normally reserved to describe God, he repeats the
exact same phrase he used some twenty years before in his prayer,
"One who perchance Is" (A, 11). He therefore indicates, first, that
man is God and, second, by the emphatic absence of the adverb
"perchance," that man is the only being whose existence is certain.
At the same time, man is not without faults and errors but, because
Zeno at this moment believes in the full potential of science and
intelligence, future progress *is* probable although man might ultimately destroy the world and himself by blowing it up or by savagely
attacking his environment in a kind of Rabelaisian science-without-
conscience syndrome. In two different passages, this ambivalent
nature is clearly exemplified: in the Ruggieri episode, Zeno looks
at himself in a prismatic mirror and sees "twenty figures compressed
and reduced . . ., twenty images of a man in a fur bonnet . . .
with gleaming eyes which were themselves mirrors" (A, 145). From
such a de-composition *en abyme* the conclusion can be drawn that
man is not only multifaceted but also that each aspect presented is
by definition an infinitely small element of the true self, hardly
visible or reconstitutable.[11] Some months later, on a Belgian dune,
he accidentally observes his eye reflected in a magnifying lens. This
experience, to which he confers the value of a symbol, shows again
human beings as "small but vast . . ., so near and yet so alien,
quick to move but vulnerable, endued with incomplete and yet
prodigious power" (A, 192), pointing to a better understanding of
the inner, dual self while stressing the idea of "multiple objects of
which he was composed" (A, 193). More interested in negating so
as to better reaffirm, Zeno has now arrived at a crucial point in his
quest for knowledge. Hiding from the Inquisition under the un-
ambiguous alias of Sébastien Gott/Theus, he leads a sedentary existence in Bruges, to which he has returned. Has he, the Wandering
Atheist, come back to his birthplace because he expects to live there
unnoticed and forgotten in the troubled times of the Counter-Ref-
ormation and nationalist upheavals, or because he is following a

preestablished orbit over which he has no control? Emese Soos does not consider Zeno's return a proof of his failure but rather an affirmation and "the completion of a cycle"[12] necessary for the self-dissolution and loss described in the *nigredo* stage of the alchemical process that would take him beyond time and space.

One of the more important chapters, "The Abyss," offers the sum of the hero's philosophy and a new beginning since in it he discovers that, in addition to the need to rid himself of all prejudices and preconceptions, he must achieve the *Selbstweiterung* Nietzsche spoke of, this broadening of the self by which one becomes integrated into the universe through understanding it. Michel Aubrion compares this "hallucinating reverie" to Pascal's meditation on the two infinites in which opposites find their full and frightening expression.[13] The dissolution and reformation of substance, required by Nicolas Flamel's double Latin imperative *solve et coagula,* "is the . . . most difficult . . ., dangerous . . ., arduous . . . part of the Great Work" (*A,* 189), for the experiment on the raw materials can only lead to *mors philosophica* in which "the operator burned by the acids of his own research, ha[s] become both subject and object, both the fragile alembic and the black precipitate" (*A,* 189).[14] In almost phenomenological fashion, everything loses its external attributes, whether Zeno thinks of his few pieces of furniture or the quill in his inkwell respectively returned to tree trunks or a goose, or of time which is a mental construct, or of place which also loses its geographical fixity (much like in Hadrian's remark about the overlapping of spatial and temporal planes [*M,* 25–26]), or of empathetic identifications with old friends, teachers, and future generations as well—apparently culminating in the daring yes spoken in contrast to a formerly equally daring no, this despite the avowed inanity and imbecility of such absolutes (*A,* 189, 177), to which dialectic Maurice Delcroix conveys a "corrosive function."[15] Zeno's "Everything was actually something else" (*A,* 187) seems to summarize very well the first phase of his "Buddhistic"[16] ascesis, until he himself concludes that there is in fact no ascent or descent but that "the abyss was both beyond the celestial sphere and within the human skull" (*A,* 193). To change opinion so often makes his character less one-dimensional, more realistic and true, and carries no notion whatever of intellectual wavering since "every philosopher changes his opinion about these things some twenty times a year" (*M,* 182).

CARNEGIE LIBRARY
LIVINGSTONE COLLEGE
SALISBURY, N. C. 28144

The friendship Zeno feels for the prior of the Franciscans provides insights into these two protagonists' minds and hearts thanks to the verbal give-and-take and the relative freedom of their conversations. The prior, a former courtier and diplomat of Emperor Charles V, is deeply anguished and tormented by the suffering of his fellowman whether at the hands of the Spanish soldiers or the Inquisition. The presence of such evil in the world and the corruption of Christian charity make him doubt at first the existence of a good and merciful God: "How many nights have I struggled against the thought that God is only a tyrant . . ., or else an impotent monarch, and that all of us, except for the atheist, who denies His very existence, utter blasphemies when we define Him" until he realizes that God is not omnipotent and cruel but is actually powerless and forsaken: He is "even weaker than we, and more discouraged still, and . . . it is our task to beget Him and save Him in all living beings" (A, 221–22). To this generous and compassionate mysticism Zeno replies that only the world of men, animals, and, maybe, plants can have feelings of misery and joy and that the spirits, like the minerals, are insentient, thereby explaining "the indifference of that immutable substance . . . we . . . call God" (A, 222).

In the Rosbo interviews, Yourcenar declares that the prior's Christian wisdom complements to a large extent Zeno's secular wisdom;[17] this is confirmed by the similar sentence both use ("It hardly matters whether a man of my age lives or dies . . ." [A, 241, 267]) to indicate that each in his way has gone beyond the white *albedo* stage, the prelate by renouncing his own sacrifice and the philosopher by understanding that he will change nothing in the grand scheme of things in which he is only a speck (A, 188), barely noticeable in the myriad moments of the universe's existence. *Albedo*, the second phase, is represented by charity and purification. Unbeknown to him until the very end, Zeno has already overcome his egotism by devoting himself to the service of others, as physician ministering to the poor, and his purification occurs on the beach at Heyst when, after deciding against fleeing to England or Holland, he takes a swim in the sea, completely naked and alone, and becomes *again* the Hermetists' Adam Kadmon "who defines and names what is inherent but undefined everywhere else in the universe" (A, 269). Cleansed by the ritual bath, this mythic Man develops into a hard and crystalline figure, entirely coherent with his acts and endowed with a wonderful and primordial ability to view himself act, think, and suffer. It would be easy to disappear into the perfect immensity that is the sea (qualifying adjectives, such as pure, truest, shadowless, ghostless, clean, prevail), but, like for Chateaubriand's René, "the hour of [his] passage had not yet sounded" (*A,* 270), and so he returns to Bruges and an obvious and more painful death.

Jailed for the wrong charge, Sébastien Theus reveals himself, as if relieved, as Zeno, the infamous author of *The Protheories* and *The Prognostications of Things to Come.* The trial that follows has all the earmarks of trials of exception of the period, except that torture is remarkably absent. The prisoner and his accusers often engage in arguments of minutely fine points of theology in which the philosopher admits readily, almost uncaringly, that "everything is magic" (*A,* 303) and, therefore, that God's will has no place in the materialist system. Sometimes, he feels quite unconcerned by the proceedings, comparing them to a card game with its admixture of lies and truths, and once even falling asleep. During the final dialogue between Zeno and his old tutor, he learns that, if he recants his apostasy, he will not be burned at the stake but sent instead to a monastery to do penance and to rehabilitate himself. He uncompromisingly refuses to retract his so-called heretical writings because these have already met with some success in less repressive circles; moreover, since any intellectual immortality he can claim will come from his readers ("his ideas had spread and taken root without him" [*A,* 279]), to reject everything would only show that his works were false and would emphasize the hypocrisy of his life. And yet he recognizes and wants to point out through another circuitous antithesis his great difficulty in saying either yes or no, for neither is a completely valid answer.[18]

Brought back to his cell, Zeno must now choose between execution to the accompaniment of the mob's jeers or suicide in calm seclusion. He has only praise for the self-imposed death of Pierre de Hamaere, the Franciscans' treasurer who, tangentially implicated in the scandal of the "Angels," "had proved capable of taking his fate in hand and of dying like a man" (*A,* 298). Thus, with hardly a hesitation, he chooses to kill himself, for, on the one hand, it means avoiding the terrifyingly painful and cruel punishment[19] and, on the other, it represents an act of lucidity and dignity. Carefully arranging the props of his death and analyzing the feelings and sensations his mind and body are experiencing, Zeno knows that "this time the act was irreversible" (*A,* 353). In a beautifully poetic

description, he hears the flowing of fountains and the roar of torrents
literally "se penser en lui" (*O*, 832; "race through him" [*A*, 354]),
and he sees the scarlet sun bleeding on the sea and climbing back
to its zenith (*A*, 354–55), both images of water and fire recalling
the two elements of human nature of which Zeno had reconfirmation
some time before (*A*, 170–72). In addition, the passage relates how
he is undergoing the last phase, the red of *rubedo*, associated with
death and with what Mircea Eliade defines as "the regression into
the amorphous, the integration into the Chaos."[20] Yourcenar drew
on the title page of her manuscript[21] various alchemical and zodiacal
signs, as well as a spiral whose unending quality seems to symbolize
her own—or anyone else's—inability to follow the hero's progress
beyond Zeno's ending: "And this is as far as one can go into the
death of Zeno" (*A*, 355). This explains why Zeno's suicide is more
than another revolt against Christian proscriptions regarding such
deeds or even the uniquely free act of the existential negator. It is
especially by sacrificing his life that he attains the supreme freedom
offered by eternity: "The anguish was over for him: he was free"
(*A*, 355).

Interestingly, unlike in Yourcenar's previous fictional works, love
as passion is mainly missing from the novel. This is not to say,
however, that Zeno or the other protagonists do not have a strong
attachment for another human being. When Zeno the student takes
up for a short while with a blond and sensual young woman, or
when the more mature wanderer finds in his friendship with his
male servant Aleï not only the wonderful secret of "a body like my
own reflecting my pleasure" (*A*, 117) but the complete absence of
affectation, lies, and flatteries usually required in more conventional
relationships, or when he spends a week in loving equality with a
widowed lady he meets in Froso, in the far north of Scandinavia
("the attributes of sex . . . counted for less than might have been
supposed, given the wisdom or follies of desire: the Lady . . . could
have been a male companion" [*A*, 183]),[22] love is presented as
being useful to combat loneliness and, sometimes, to channel a
surfeit of tenderness. Although Aleï's death caused Zeno great sadness and brought him to the point of tears, such a strong emotion
as love may not be possible for him for two important reasons: one,
his status as questioner of established ideas forces him to be always
on the run and thus unable to develop more lasting feelings; two,
his affirmation, outside any order or cult, of the individual qua

rational makes him interested in the intellect rather than the emotion, and sex, too, despite its "burning mysteries," assumes the value of a physical experience "for the philosopher to try, but then to renounce thereafter" (*A,* 191). To the more convenient homosexuality of a wandering Zeno, Henri-Maximilien offers a valiant defense of heterosexual love, and yet he cannot help but heave a sigh of relief whenever he leaves a mistress, because his conception of love, based on Platonic beauty, fulfills an ideal found only in art and literature. Except for the prior and Zeno, the other characters do not testify to an excess of true and unselfish amity for one another, whether they are married or not. Affection, let alone love, is in fact a rare commodity in *The Abyss.* Even Martha, while apparently loving her cousin Bénédicte with an angelic love, cannot long sustain her friendship in the face of the deaths caused by the plague of 1549. Now that Bénédicte has been struck by the disease, a terrified Martha sees in her "an enemy, an animal, a dangerous object" (*A,* 97) who, by this very malady, has become the Other, prefiguring her future and, above all, reminding her of her own fragile animal condition.[23] Martha's fear and dastardliness are particularly evident here when she makes it a point to accurately state the exact relationship that exists between them and to effectively separate herself from the dying girl: "I am not her sister . . . I am her cousin" (*A,* 98), as if death might mistakenly come for her, to which Zeno perspicaciously responds that shame and remorse can be considered as evil as the black plague itself. (This same "fatal vice" [*A,* 323] of cowardice will cause the repudiation, in a chapter satirically titled "A Noble Abode," of Martha's connection with her half-brother and therefore prevent a possible reprieve of his punishment.) Simon Adriansen, Martha's father, to the contrary, is so loving and self-sacrificing that he is easily taken advantage of by his debtors, his co-religionists, and finally by his wife. After her adultery and death in Münster, he is willing to forgive everything and everyone, and since nothing matters anymore, he goes as far as to renounce the naive tenets of his faith in one last bittersweet act: "Something told him that the Eternal no longer asked him to pray" (*A,* 81–82).

To construct this rich fresco of sixteenth-century Europe, Yourcenar was faced with different problems from those of her contemporary novels and especially from *Memoirs of Hadrian.* Again, she refused outright to create local color by the abuse of quaintness usually found in historical fiction, although, of course, her characters

live and die according to the requirements of the moment. Yourcenar
has increased the action's realism both by using authentic events
found in historical and biographical sources which she has then
modified or adapted to suit the needs of the plot and the truth of
the psychology, and by having period figures appear, participate,
and speak in her work, much like Walter Scott or Honoré de Balzac
before her. In this manner, we find among the four hundred people
of *L'Oeuvre au noir* such personages as Christian and Arab rulers, the
leaders of the Münster rebellion, two queens (Margaret of Austria
and Catherine de' Medici) who intervene directly in the story. Because more documents of all kinds, including interrogation tran-
scripts recorded at various trials of exception,[24] exist relating the
voice and tone of everyday language and speech for the sixteenth
century than for the second, it was easier for the author to convey
thoughts appropriate to the Renaissance, as well as to re-create
conversations of the past which she hoped would be "plausible."[25]
Thus, the indirect style—conjugated in the imperfect indicative,
instead of the customary simple past—which she qualifies as a
"monologue in the third person singular" (*Y,* 62) is in a sense a
modified version of the "portrait of a voice"; now, as in her earlier
texts, this narrative technique allows her to understand better her
unique characters and, consequently, to attain and reveal "the human
and the universal" (*Y,* 62).

    Yourcenar's magnificent novel of the human spirit, slowly ma-
tured from her early discovery of old family papers bearing strange
names like Hilzonde, Zénon, and Vivine, names that made her
dream and fired her imagination[26] into the original short story dated
1934, became an instant popular success upon its publication in
1968, a year famous for other forms of conflicts and questionings.
Awarded the Fémina Prize in an unprecedented unanimous first-
ballot vote and translated into eighteen languages, it was praised
by most critics. Jean Onimus, for example, underlines the dark and
violent "picture of human stupidity, of injustice and of fundamental
chaos," to which Sophie Deroisin adds: "We see . . . a long, tragic
contemplation of life; the unceasing gifts of poetry and imagination
enliven a work beaten by the great confused waves of History."
Gonzague Truc, too, calls *The Abyss* an exciting and passionate novel
of history and ideas. For her part, despite reservations regarding
Yourcenar's "artificial" rendering of the period, Gennie Luccioni
writes that the book is fascinating, especially in its realistic descrip-

tion *à la* Hieronymus Bosch of an autopsy and of the ravages of the plague. Whereas Henri Clouard finds some of Zeno's discussions and musings, along with the narrator's explanations, to be heavy-handed and boring, Robert Kanters, in two separate reviews, assesses the merits of the novel in glowing terms: "A master book. One of these very rare works . . . like a vast forest or a temple" that "takes man's bearings at the time when . . . the dawn of knowledge and science is rising."[27]

In illustrating and analyzing her hero's difficult progress, Yourcenar has shown that any seeker of truth, by definition, acts as a defier of established, and Establishment, values and must perforce be destroyed by the right-thinking defenders of the *status quo* ("Whoever is not like them is against them" [*A, 109*]). After having already exposed in *A Coin in Nine Hands* and *Memoirs of Hadrian* the dangers extant in our modern world, she can only deplore once again "with indignant innocence"[28] the bleak visage presented by man, so easily capable of violence and evil against his neighbor and against nature. It is not surprising, then, that Zeno would much prefer death with "animo e stile" ("heart and bearing" [Julian de' Medici epigraph, *A, 289*]) to life in horror of the human condition.

Chapter Five

The Autobiographical Works

Marguerite Yourcenar's autobiographical writings show the same preoccupations, themes, and techniques as her novels and short stories. The presentation in *Feux* of the torments caused by love, however, together with interpretations of ancient legends, allows more direct access to the understanding of her affective qualities. In *Les Songes et les sorts,* exploration of her oneiric world provides fascinating insights into her subconscious mind, and in *Le Labyrinthe du Monde*[1] the narration of her parental histories demonstrates again the unending ties that unite man to his fellowman, what Yourcenar calls "the human dough" (*Y,* 217).

Feux

The discussion of *Feux* (*Fires,* 1936) may seem more appropriate elsewhere in this study due to its combination of poetry and lyrical prose;[2] yet it is also autobiographical in nature, as Yourcenar herself has hinted on several occasions. Because she relies on entries from her private diaries to convey the tragic complaint of "a love *(passionnelle)* crisis," her "pensées" (*F,* x) serve, thanks to the immense scope of her culture and knowledge of antiquity, as the inspiration for associations and connections that link her own passion to those found in Greek and biblical myths and stories.

Fires relates the course of a love affair from its beginning happiness to anger and despair at being abandoned, from hope for the loved one's return coupled with renewed discovery of passion to resignation in light of repeated failures and final self-assertion.

The birth of love sets Yourcenar apart from mere mortals: *"I don't believe as they do, I don't live as they do, I don't love as they do"* (*F,* 4), and brings such a surfeit of joy that the lover fills the entire universe and takes on the concentrated qualities of heavy metals (*F,* 3). At the same time, the story of Phaedra already points to the destructiveness of mad love since hers has brought about Hippolytus' death and Theseus' loss; her final words ("Thank you" [*F,* 9]) give an ironic twist to her misery, as well as emphasize that the torture she endured, the hypocrisy she lived with and her own death—all were worth it. The author, still flying high (*"On a plane, next to you, I am no longer afraid"* [F, 10]) and indestructible in the face of death, which comes only for those seeking it out, will challenge death to find her by hiding in secret passageways and under trap doors: *"Death, to kill me, will need me as an accomplice"* (F, 11).

In the next parable, Achilles has disguised himself as a young woman the better to avoid recognition by his compatriots and enlistment in the Trojan War. Out of jealousy of the feminine Deidamia whom Patroclus seems to favor, he kills her and, guided by the masculine Misandra, runs away, also through hidden doors and staircases, to meet his destiny. The murder of the feminine princess and the escape aided by her masculine cousin, as Frederick and Edith Farrell have demonstrated, symbolize the two aspects of Achilles' nature;[3] by choosing the virile half, he is finally able to reject all his lies and become the god he always wanted to be: "Ashamed not to have recognized in the kings the secret emissaries of his own courage, certain to have let slip his only chance to be a god, . . . Achilles started walking on this fated cable [and from] this disheveled girl . . . a god was emerging" (F, 19, 21–22).

Patroclus, along with many great heroes, is dead in the next narrative, and a despondent Achilles fights all enemies as if they were not humans. When the Amazons come in droves over the horizon, his fury reaches its height, for "all his life, Achilles had taken women to represent the instinctive part of misfortune, the one he did not choose but had to endure and couldn't accept" (F, 30). Only Penthesilea, from among them, can be the equal "worthy to be a [male] friend" (F, 32) since she represents a masculine principle devoid of all living essence (carapaced, helmeted, gold, mineral are terms used to describe her) and even the hand-to-hand duel, compared to a well choreographed Ballet Russe, assumes the spatial quality of motion and the elusive illusion of death. This is why the narrator's statement, *"Where shall I run to? You fill the world. I can only escape you in you"* (F, 23), is echoed in the story's last sentence: "[Penthesilea] was the only creature in the world who looked[4] like Patroclus" (F, 32).

Yourcenar's love is so great that she loses herself in her adoration and carries in her womb a monstrous offspring of terrible pain at the adored's leaving and the awful incertitude of being loved one day and scorned the next ("*drunk with happiness*" in contrast to "*glutted with unhappiness*" [*F*, 24]). Antigone chooses to bury Polynices, in whom she sees the absence of fraud and the aura of honor, because her uncompromising quest for an ideal and her love of justice have fated her to die. By her example, she helps Yourcenar to bear the unbearable feelings of abandonment: "All suffering yielded to changes into serenity" (*F*, 38), declares the storyteller, and the persona of the *pensées* adds hesitatingly, though hopefully, "*One reaches all great events of life a virgin. I am afraid of not knowing how to deal with suffering*" (*F*, 44). On the other hand, the abused victim, Lena, teaches that suffering and mistreatment can be tolerated if no one knows the secret of her humiliation (*F*, 60), a lesson not lost on the author: " '*Burned with more fires . . .' Worn-out beast . . . a hot whip lashes my back . . . I wake up each night with my own blood ablaze . . . I hope this book will never be read*" (*F*, 61, 3).

Along with the beloved's return and the euphoric renewal of the liaison, "*everything becomes limpid again . . . No, you are not going: I am keeping you . . . I entrust myself to this terrible airplane propelled by a heart . . . Ah, to die in order to stop Time*" (*F*, 78–80), Mary Magdalene's autobiographical monologue which serves to explain how she found salvation from her physical, mental, and spiritual debauchery through her complete abnegation and her love of Christ, Yourcenar also realizes that "*I had to love you to understand that the most mediocre or the worst of human beings is worthy, up there, of inspiring God's eternal sacrifice*" (*F*, 80).

Phaedo's search for wisdom and knowledge finds its fulfillment in the vertiginous dancing he executes at the end of his tale. While he has danced already twice before, it is only now that his consummate art makes him invisible, that his supreme speed renders even death immobile, and that his immense parabolas circumscribe the entire universe, from man-made cities to the sea below and the stars above. Thanks to his wondrous performance he is able to negate all human absolutes and finally to "erase all memories and abolish all forms."[5] For Yourcenar, too, there is a similar cosmic—and orgasmic—flight as her "*pleasure executes a forced landing in midair, the sound of its engines frenzied by the heart's last somersaults*" (*F*, 98).

In her deposition to the judges, Clytemnestra readily admits her murder of Agamemnon, yet her guilt is mitigated by his behavior. After a ten-year absence, he has returned home only to act as though nothing had happened. He shakes Aegisthus' hand, hardly looks at his wife, makes jokes about cuckolds and unfaithful women, and caresses a young Turkish girl brought back from the war. Not a word about Clytemnestra's adultery, no outburst of anger: he ignores her completely, and this is the reason why she has had to kill him— to prove that she existed and "to force him to realize that I was not a thing of no importance" (*F,* 110). She has been unable, however, to find peace in her crime as her husband's ghost haunts her day and night; she knows that she will again and again fall in love with her dead husband, that this will only lead to his repeated leaving, and that she will have to go on murdering him forever. Trapped in this web of violence, she can only put her dilemma to her judges: "What can I do? You can't kill a dead man" (*F,* 112). Like Clytemnestra, Yourcenar feels that she also is being taken for granted by the one she loves (*"Not to be loved anymore is to become invisible; now you don't notice that I have a body"* [*F,* 113])—quite the contrary to what she herself refused to do: *"I won't allow myself to turn you into an object, even into the Beloved Object"* (*F,* 33).

"Sappho, or Suicide" is the last story of the work. In this modern transposition, Sappho is no longer a poetess but a talented circus acrobat, caught between earth and sky, savoring the pleasure of flight and the thrill of danger. She loves Attys passionately, who abandons her to return to her boy friend. Sappho, in searching for her in all the dingy towns on her tour, finds Phaon who reminds her so much of Attys: same mouth, same forehead, same eyes. When he appears in her bedroom dressed in Attys' negligee, she understands that the happiness of love will again be followed by abandonment and despair in a never-ending cycle of affairs. Having decided to kill herself Sappho swings higher and higher on her trapeze, but she fails at her attempt and falls instead into the safety net. Therefore, by transcending her own physical limitations ("she can continue to surpass herself by bursting through her sky . . . her fate now mastered" [*F,* 128]), she can save herself and be reborn through her art much as Wang-Fô had done in his final painting. From this, Yourcenar learns that suicide is ultimately pointless: *"I will not kill myself. The dead are so quickly forgotten"* (*F,* 130) and, after taking full responsibility for her life, she at last wishes to take "a personal experience to its farthest possible point and . . . to end by going beyond it":[6] *"It's not a question of suicide. It's only a question of beating a record"* (*F,* 130).

Yourcenar's *Fires* is "an entirely burning book" (*Y*, 97) whose personal observations and mythic illustrations propose not only "theorems of passion" but also reveal to the most careful reader a secret world, an inner universe which hides "the most disquieting of masked balls—the one where someone disguises himself as HIM-SELF."[7] It is no wonder, then, that Yourcenar calls this costume ball "a stage of [my] awareness" (*F*, xxii).

Les Songes et les sorts

Two years after *Feux*, Marguerite Yourcenar published *Les Songes et les sorts* (Dreams and fates, 1938), a collection of narratives describing the dreams she experienced between her twenty-eighth and thirty-third year, including several recurring dreams from her childhood and young adolescence. Although she does not fully subscribe to Freudian theories of dreams since she was writing "quite apart from psychological trends,"[8] there are enough buildings (e.g., houses, rooms, churches, palaces, caves, etc.), standing and fallen trees, white and red flowers, dark tunnels and corridors, flowing and crusted blood, still-born and sickly infants, clear and stagnant waters, as well as other symbolic characters, objects, places, and situations, to allow for a broad spectrum of fascinating Freudian interpretations. This is not her aim, however,[9] because on the one hand such interpretations are insufficient and unsatisfying, and on the other because she is interested in the aesthetic of the oneiric world, especially "at the moment when fates express themselves through dreams" (*S*, 13), rather than in a psychological explanation of the dreamer's subconscious.

Deliberately omitting physiological and sexual dreams for their common banality, she herself classifies her twenty-one episodes into eight categories (*S*, 8–10): (1) memory of her dead father; (2) ambition and pride; (3) terror and fright; (4) search for a lost woman; (5) death; (6) church/cathedral (open or closed); (7) pond; and (8) love. Of course, several motifs, plots, and locales may occur in one dream. Of these dream categories, the following discussion will focus on the themes of the quest for a lost woman, love, and death.

There are four main *songes* in which Yourcenar relates her search for a woman who often disappears from her. Sometimes this woman is given the dual role of witness, staring "with the dense and impenetrable fixity of stones" (*S,* 167), and of mother forever cradling in her arms a still-born or moribund baby; this maternal personage is particularly evident in a dream entitled "Les Cierges dans la cathédrale" (Candles in the cathedral). Tall, young, beautiful, majestic, clothed in heavy skirts, she is referred to as "goddess . . . mother, or rather *mothers,* in the plural" (*S,* 124–25) since she is at once the epitome and the nexus of all mothers. A presentation of a lost—and pitiless—woman is given in "Les Clefs de l'église" (The keys of the church; both of these also fit within category 6) where a young gypsy girl, in contrast to the stately goddess, is half naked, frail, and emaciated and looks at Yourcenar "with teeth clenched . . . and an air of anxious defiance" (*S,* 87); immediately she reminds the dreamer of another: "I no longer see anything . . . but her eyes, her blue eyes, her immense eyes, her admirable eyes that belong to someone else" (*S,* 87).

In other dreams, the woman is the accomplice or mistress of Yourcenar's lover. This more or less innocent ménage à trois occurs in three texts in particular. Here, love is obviously the main theme. The lover, whose dream age ranges between adolescence and young manhood, is described either as an unfeeling cad or a fearless rescuer of damsels in distress. She is usually very understanding of her rival, for instance, of "the young girl who cries" and who shares the same man. The teary-eyed girl has brought some flowers and a letter for him which, upon his return, he angrily tears up as "he . . . gets ready to lie as a musician gets ready to play" (*S,* 209). This lying, cheating nature of his is an important aspect of all the author's mature dreams; she constantly sought to uncover the reality and truth beneath his beautiful veneer, to find the hidden name which she sensed to be truly descriptive of his insensitivity: "I know . . . that this name is that of the man I have loved, his true name, the one he does not bear in life and which I did not know until this day" (*S,* 49); "I recognize under this disguise . . . the man I have loved so much and so dearly" (*S,* 168); "I would give what little I have . . . to remove from him this face as one removes a mask" (*S,* 214); "this simple rubbing is enough to remove from this dense and hard body all traces of humanity" (*S,* 218). As rescuer, he is both brave and assertive, often liberating the dreaming heroine from a fate worse than death, as in "Les Coeurs arrachés" (Torn-out hearts) and "La Maison des femmes pâles" (The house of pale women): "He takes me by the hand. We go out of the bedroom, we walk downstairs by a concealed staircase . . ." (S, 169), and in "La Maison brûlée" (The burned house), where he leads her away from the "very dangerous" Cyrille. Nonetheless, it is as a cruel lover, uncaring about her suffering, that he figures most prominently in her dreams, and even the times in which he appears dead or dying (Freud, no doubt, would have interpreted these as wish-fulfillments) give very little relief to her battered heart.

Finally, death plays the most important role in the collection. Whether Yourcenar speaks of the results (i.e., dead father, infant, lover, animal, flower) or of the dramatis persona Death, with a capital D, she has the greatest reverence for what she calls "this great black certainty" (S, 9). Indeed, powerful suicidal attractions are described in such dreams as "La Route sous la neige" (The road under the snow), "Les Chevaux sauvages" (The wild horses), and "Les Caisses à fleurs" (The flowerboxes). Death in the form of murder also appears: lest the curate's servant poison her ("I must kill her to prevent her from making me die" [S, 181]), she throws a knife into her heart, and the servant literally vanishes into the wallpaper, leaving the dreamer with an odd, even unsettling feeling of non-accomplishment. (This is also an example of the lost-woman category.) In "La Flaque dans l'église" (The puddle in the church), Death is a full-fledged character who plays the cello in the cloister's gardens and is surrounded by a suite of ladies-in-waiting who all wear gowns of different colors. Yourcenar refuses to be tempted into joining them, not out of discourtesy, but because "I have on my everyday clothes and I am in a hurry" (S, 156). In the last scene, the cello is replaced by an organ, both instruments being associated in her mind with love.[10] She therefore continues here the archetypal tradition that equates love with death.

The most frightening nightmare, however, and one of the few that has its origins in Yourcenar's childhood, is "La Mare maudite" (The cursed pool; also from category 7). Its very title reveals the horror of the symbol. Whereas her other images usually have appealing characteristics, the "invitation to suicide" (S, 53) of this Ophelia-complex tale is proffered in the bleakest and most oppressive terms (lead-colored pond, stunted trees, malevolent plants, dirty white, dingy and low sky, colorless pond that seems forever poisoned, baneful little pool) which seem to sound echoes of the Baudelairean spleen.

Dreams, of course, also take place in her novels, for example, in *La Nouvelle Eurydice, Mémoires d'Hadrien, L'Oeuvre au noir,* and *Denier du rêve,* this last title pointing out so well her allegorical interests despite the plot's realistic roots in Fascist Italy. In *Les Songes et les sorts,* as well as in Yourcenar's fiction, the dreamer, much like Narcissus, finds in his dream the symbolic reflection of himself, and thus he can sometimes use it to predict the future since the oneiric world is at the junction of the past and present forces within him. To a large extent, it is this destiny, this fatality, these *sorts* that are expressed in the second part of the book's title—a concept she explained in an interview: "The fates, in the sense of 'lot,' the 'lot' of an individual. . . . The lots that fall to you. There are surely relationships between the destiny of a being and his dreams. There is something magical in the dream, if by magic we understand unexplained associations" (*Y,* 110). By thus emphasizing the omnipotent force of Destiny, she seems to reject, as Jean Blot has suggested, man's free will while, at the same time, doubting his innocence or at least his guiltlessness.[11]

In order to accomplish her goal Yourcenar has built a gloomy, closed universe filled with towers and cells not unlike that world drawn by Piranesi (about whom she wrote an essay published in her *Sous bénéfice d'inventaire*). The colors she uses are either ice-cold gray and white or blood red, although blue is sometimes used also; the atmosphere is mostly stifling, airless, destructive, and the action gripping, tragic, even pathetic. Above all, she wants to allow the reader "to weigh the imponderable, to introduce himself through the reversal of analogies . . . into the very center of a foreign world, finally to acclimate himself each time . . . to the new and bizarre odor of dreams" (*S,* 135), and to glimpse into her soul[12] by availing himself of a few chapters from the "Memoirs of my dreamed life" (*S,* 34). And until the publication of *Le Labyrinthe du Monde* (*Souvenirs pieux* and *Archives du Nord*), this series had indeed provided the most important access to Marguerite Yourcenar's deeply private other world.

Le Labyrinthe du Monde

When Michel Foucault declared in his inaugural lecture at the Collège de France, "One asks [the author] to reveal, or at least bring before him, the hidden sense that goes through [his works]; one asks him to hinge them on his personal life and his lived experiences, on the real history which saw them born,"[13] he was only stating what the reading public, from the beginning of literature, has wanted from its writers, namely, to gain an insight into the author's mind and imagination. In response, writers kindly obliged by narrating their life story, and a new genre was born.

Whether autobiographies are considered explanations of their authors' lives, or justifications of past behavior and events, they all try, according to Philippe Lejeune, "to seize one's person in its totality, in a movement which recapitulates the synthesis of the 'me.' "[14] It is, of course, the focusing on the self that is fascinating to the reader, even when the portrait is viewed as not quite truthful. This is why many writings include the word "truth" or some such synonymous expression in their titles: *Dichtung und Wahrheit* (Goethe), *Mon coeur mis à nu* (Baudelaire), *Si je mens* (F. Giroud), *My Truth* (I. Gandhi). This "vouloir-être-sincère-avec-moi" (in Paul Valéry's phrase) is at the basis of every autobiographical work, and even if the author does not succeed in this worthy endeavor, he still has revealed much that is hidden in his character, for the act of lying or of disguising the truth is also part of his persona, real or mythical.

Before turning to Yourcenar's two-volume autobiography, let us consider the question, What is an autobiography? Roy Pascal, in his classic American study, *Design and Truth in Autobiography,* answers by stating that it is "an interplay, a collusion, between past and present; its significance is indeed more the revelation of the present situation than the uncovering of the past." This view is shared by Louis Renza, who states: "Autobiography is the writer's attempt to elucidate his present, not his past." On the other hand, James Olney argues that it is "among other things, a point of view on the writer's own past life . . . , a metaphor of one's own self." Lejeune provides the most all-encompassing definition, worthy of an excellent dictionary: "[Autobiography is a] retrospective narrative in prose that a real person makes of his own existence when he puts the accent on his individual life, in particular on the story of his personality"; this is itself an amplification of the axiom postulated by Jean Starobinski: "The biography of a person done by himself."[15] The originality of Yourcenar's *Le Labyrinthe du Monde* (The labyrinth of the world, 1974 and 1977) is that she has not only questioned in her book the definitions and theories of the autobiographical genre but she has ignored the traditional rules as well, thus writing a modern anti-autobiography.

The author begins her life story commonly enough with her birth:

> The being which I call me came into the world a certain Monday, 8 June 1903, around eight in the morning, in Brussels, born to a Frenchman belonging to an old Northern family and a Belgian woman whose ancestors had been over several centuries established in Liège, then settled in the Hainaut. The house where this event occurred, since every birth is one for the father and the mother and the few people who are close to them, was located at 193 Avenue Louise, and disappeared some fifteen years ago, devoured by a building. (*SP*, 11)

But unlike other autobiographies, hers does not dwell on her childhood, that special period of love and hatred, of pleasure and pain, of charm and terror, and ultimately that state of *tabula rasa* on which experiences and feelings will inscribe what will become the writer. Instead of telling about *her* life, *her* works, *her* assorted great deeds usually found in such writings, she evokes in the first volume, *Souvenirs pieux* (Holy memorial cards), the history of her mother and her mother's ancestors, and in the second, *Archives du Nord* (Northern archives), that of her father and his forebears. Each branch of the family is described in a different historiographical style: the maternal side by going backward and stopping at each generational level to the Belle Epoque, the Belgium of the nineteenth century, to rococo and medieval Liège, and even "as far as the Roman times, or pre-Roman" (*AN*, 13). The paternal ascendance, on the contrary, is portrayed by starting in "the night of time" (*AN*, 11) and working up to the Lille of the nineteenth century and to the man who was to become her father. Thus, she is both the heir of these two ancient blood lines and the *ultima summa* of an immense, almost universal ancestry.

As Theseus met with his destiny in *Qui n'a pas son Minotaure?*, Marguerite Yourcenar must also discover within her personal, awesome labyrinth ("sinister sides," "eternal chambers of horror")[16] the wonderful intelligence that makes her the unique character of and victor over her own life. It is not surprising, then, that she entered this world, her blue eyes wide open, "cry[ing] with full lungs, trying her strength, already manifesting that terrible vitality which fills each being" (*SP*, 28), and knowing that "all knowledge, whatever it is, takes us back to ourselves, because it came from us."[17]

At the age of thirty-five, she had already "often thought to write one day a volume of intimate memoirs: some scruples . . . deter me in advance from this project which only the strongest soul . . . could execute without lies" (*S,* 142).[18] To accomplish this painstaking task without lying, Yourcenar purposely relies on family documents, photographs, oral narratives, and relics, as well as on library archives at Lille, Versailles, and Ghent, in order to present much more than her genealogical roots.

Unafraid to show the selfishness of her aristocratic class (she was born de Crayencour) or the meanness of her paternal grandmother who, on learning that her daughter-in-law was dying of puerperal fever, tactlessly inquired: "You don't think I could catch this illness?" (*SP,* 38), and unawed by the empty blandishments of this world, she has refused to transform her ancestors into mythic heroes and heroines.

Her father, who had the word "anankê" tatooed on his left arm, was consistently at odds with Fate. A nonconformist from his early childhood on, at age fifteen, he ran away from his mother, "the intolerable Noémi," and his henpecked father "in whom his son wants to see only, rightly or wrongly, one of these burdened and conciliatory husbands which he promised himself not to be in his turn" (*AN,* 241), to vainly try to become a cabin boy on any cargo ship sailing for the Far East or Australia. After enlisting in the French army and deserting twice, he temporarily settled down in Brussels with his second wife, Yourcenar's mother. While Yourcenar loves this "free man, perhaps the freest man I have known: he did what he believed right, what he believed must be done, what he believed he loved to do,"[19] she has obvious ambivalent feelings toward her mother: on the one hand, she admires Fernande for having so scandalously flouted upper-class morality by going on an "engagement trip" with her future husband (*SP,* 274), and on the other, she resents her for having tried, almost from beyond the grave, to "encroach unduly on my life and my own liberty" by recommending in her last breath: "If the little one ever wants to be a nun, don't anyone prevent her" (*SP,* 43).

Thus, by presenting "the reality of a given individual at a given moment,"[20] Yourcenar has painted her family, warts and all ("We must have the courage to look at people from the past as we look at our contemporaries . . . without ever making them into idols or statues"),[21] with all the minute carefulness and precision of the historian. This does not mean, however, that dialogues should be taken as verbatim transcriptions of actually held conversations, for "anyone who claims to remember a conversation word for word has always struck me as a mythomaniac, or a liar" (*CG,* 90) or that the undocumented events could not have taken place (for instance, the meeting and subsequent love feeling between Yourcenar's great-great-grandmother Anne-Marie and the French revolutionary leader, Saint-Just), as long as these hypothetical occurrences are both symbolically revealing and psychologically accurate.

Her goal, therefore, is to present the image of her own self, of a human being living with all her complexity and history, what Georges Gusdorf calls "one's testimonies upon oneself and signs of the new impassioned disquiet of modern man, relentless to elucidate the mysteries of his own personality."[22] To understand why "the incidents of this life interest [her] above all as the access roads by which certain experiences touched her" (*AN,* 373), Yourcenar must descend deeper into the past, beyond her own actual birth since, like Baudelaire, she has "more memories than if I were a thousand years old": "Like most new-born humans, she appears to be a very old being who is going to rejuvenate. And, in fact, she is very old: either by the ancestral blood and genes or by the unanalyzed element which, by a beautiful and ancient metaphor, we call the soul, she has crossed the centuries" (*AN,* 370).

In this historical construct, in addition to her desire to achieve the Stendhalian *parfaite sincérité,* she is also interested in re-creating a world, a society and its mores, a cast of characters that, almost in predestinarian fashion ("the essential is in us from the beginning"),[23] have helped in shaping the author. Whether it is the original Cleenewerk of the early 1500s, "comfortably settled on his plot of earth . . . and buried, his time come, in his parish, to the noise of a high mass" (*AN,* 37) or the Quartiers (later spelled Cartier) who were governors of the city of Liège from 1366 on, all of whom, through marriage, influence, and high positions, acquired land, wealth and titles, even during the bloody days of the Terror (*SP,* 63–100), Yourcenar strives to bring to life those influences which have acted upon her.

She suggests in volume 1 what is required in order to give life to the past: "Passed life is a dry leaf, crackled, without sap or chlorophyl, riddled with holes, scratched with tears, which, held against the light, offers no more than the skeletal network of its

thin and broken nervures. Certain efforts are required to return to
it the fleshy and green aspect of a fresh leaf, to restore to events or
incidents that fullness which fulfills those who live them and prevents them from imagining other things" (*SP,* 110). Yet she completely rejects the banal stereotypes normally found in such re-
creations. She knows that the history of humanity is necessarily her
own history and that, like Montaigne, not only does she carry within
her genes and psyche "the entire form of the human condition"[24]
but also that "finally one inherits a world, and that is what interests
me. One feels oneself a moment of passage, quite accidental, in the
series of generations."[25] She thereby rejoins the biographies of her
own Roman Emperor Hadrian and her Flemish philosopher Zeno,
who, as a matter of fact, appears briefly in *Archives du Nord* (48)
and in *Souvenirs pieux* ("I love Zeno like a brother" [217]).

At the same time, Yourcenar's autobiography can be considered
a "meditation upon history" (to quote William Styron) in the sense
that she also deals with universal human problems, ranging from
air and water pollution to the conscious rape of the land, from
overpopulation to the wanton destruction of elephants and baby
seals:

Above her cradle swings an ivory cross. . . . The ivory comes from an
elephant killed in the Congolese forest. . . . This great mass of intelligent
life, issue of a dynasty which goes back at least as far as the beginning of
the Pleistocene Period, ended in that. This gewgaw was part of an animal
who grazed the grasses and drank the river waters, who bathed in the
good, warm mud, who used this ivory to battle a rival or to try to parry
the attacks of man, who flattered with his trunk the female with whom
he used to couple. (*SP,* 29)

Although she is aware that her Shandean-like digressions may appear
to some readers as highly sentimentalized flights of fancy and worth-
less nonsense ("certain readers of this book without doubt will find
this remark [with regard to the milk cows] and those which precede
equally ridiculous" [*SP,* 31]), these comments reveal more than the
depth of Yourcenar's concern over and feelings about her world.
They also underline the basically pessimistic outlook of her thought:
"What dances today on the earth is the foolishness, the violence,
and the greediness of man" (*AN,* 371–72).

The intermediate link between the past and the future, carrier of
a special destiny which binds all human beings together, she comes

to the realization that "my face begins to draw itself on the screen of time" (*SP*, 297)—a face she has promised to flesh out in her still-to-be-published volume 3 that will borrow its title from a Rimbaud line, "Quoi, l'éternité?" ("L'Eternité," in *Derniers Vers*).

Because, like Proust, she deeply believes that the past is not only recaptured but also redeemed, her autobiography is ultimately an attempt to rescue her ascendants from the accumulated dust of family and municipal archives. More than the turn-of-the-century *souvenirs pieux*—those saccharine images eulogizing the dead—Marguerite Yourcenar has succeeded in commemorating and immortalizing her ancestors' memories and thereby saving them from oblivion. Furthermore, she has gone far back into man's past, beyond the "high tides immemorial" (*AN*, 14) and found for herself the peace and perpetual life promised by the religious mourning cards: "Je m'associe, infime, à cette immensité;/Je goûte, en vous voyant, ma part d'éternité."[26]

Chapter Six

Writings of Diverse Genres

Marguerite Yourcenar is most famous for her novels, but she has written, as we have already seen, in other genres as well. This chapter will deal first with her short stories, followed by a discussion of her drama, poetry, translations, and, finally, essays.

Short Stories

La Mort conduit l'attelage (Death drives the team, 1934) is a collection of three stories,[1] set in the sixteenth and seventeenth centuries, which present different aspects of a world in the manner of a particular painter: "D'après Dürer," "D'après Greco," "D'après Rembrandt." "D'après Dürer" became *L'Oeuvre au noir* of 1968, while the El Greco and Rembrandt narratives were partially rewritten, the El Greco appearing in 1981 as a separate volume entitled *Anna, soror . . .* (Anna, sister . . .), and the Rembrandt completely reworked ("not a line of it remains, but it contained . . . within it seeds which ended by germinating")[2] to make two related stories, "Un Homme obscur" (An obscure man) and "Une Belle Matinée" (A beautiful morning). These three texts were then published together under the general title of *Comme l'eau qui coule* (Like flowing water) in 1982.

Anna, soror . . . is a gripping tale which, like the Spanish master's haunting paintings, is intense and corrosive. The burning incestuous passion with which Don Miguel de La Cena and his sister are driven toward one another is told with considerable self-restraint, ever so delicately, much like the slow dance performed by Anna's feet in her brother's dream.

It is in the late Renaissance, and Miguel and his sister are slowly bringing back to Spanish-held Naples the coffin of their mother. The journey is made even longer in the stifling heat of the summer and the constant threat of pestilence. It is in this unbearable climate that they seek each other out at the same time that they shun each other. This avoidance cannot be successful, however, given the closed, almost claustrophobic environment of the carriage. "He sat crammed in his corner, the farthest away from her possible. . . . The bumps threw them against each other" (*O*, 868), and when Anna faints from exhaustion and the general airlessness, he cannot prevent himself from administering to her, especially since her maid is slow in coming: "He unlaced her; he looked anxiously for the place of her heart; the heartbeats resumed under his fingers" (*O*, 868). This obviously Good Samaritan and humane act is nevertheless viewed by Miguel with such horror that he first insists the maid stay with them during the remainder of the trip home and then, not unlike Lady Macbeth, he "continually rubs one hand against the other as if to blot something out" (*O*, 869).

Brother and sister spend their days in the conscious sublimation of their feelings through prayers and holy readings, and the young man, drained from sleepless nights and pent-up emotion, learns to recognize his passion, which until then he had not dared name and from which he thought he had been the first ever to suffer. This knowledge, rather than helping to relieve his sick mind, adds to his torture. Instead of searching for renewed patience toward his sister, he turns on her in the most cruel fashion. It is as though Eros has revealed his true face with a sadistic behavior that is punishing both the victim and the tormentor. He speaks to her harshly, he reproaches her constantly, he finds fault with everything she does or says. In her turn, she can only accept his chastising in silence and cry at night "asking herself how she could have offended him" (*O*, 871).

Months go by during which he tries to delude himself in myriad debauches and she in prayerful meditation, but to no avail. So they devour each other, not knowing where they are going, except that, as he fights against his desire and his scruples, he is beginning to hate her while still loving her passionately, feverishly, even sacrilegiously: "And you would live [in a convent], drenched by tears, consuming yourself with love for a wax figure? . . . I would permit you a lover just because he is crucified? . . . Do you believe that I want to surrender you to God? . . . Never!" (*O*, 880).

Anna finally understands his conduct when she reads the biblical passage mentioned by Miguel in which Amnon implores his sister Tamar ("Come to bed with me, sister. . . . He would not listen, but overpowered her, dishonored her, and raped her" [2 Samuel 13]) and hears the irresistible excitement of her heart, as she decides to go to her brother's room: "He approached his door . . . and ended by leaning against it. He felt she was leaning against it too; the trembling of their two bodies spread to the woodwork. . . . Each listened . . . to the panting of a desire similar to his own. She dared not beg him to open. To dare to open, he waited for her to speak" (*O*, 881). On the night of Good Friday, with the sky "resplendent with wounds"—both indications reminding the reader of the crucifixion of Christ and of El Greco's *View of Toledo*—Anna asked:

> Why did you not kill me, my brother?
> I thought of it, he said. I would love you dead. (*O*, 883)

It was that night that they became lovers. Miguel pays for his act with his life, Anna with a loveless marriage, since love—any kind of love—is a crime for which punishment must always be exacted, although neither protagonist is repentant: "Having nothing more to expect from life, he rushed toward death as toward a necessary conclusion" (*O*, 884), while she murmured in her dying breath, "Mi amado . . ." ("My beloved" [*O*, 901]).[3]

"Existence," declares Jean Blot, "is only a mask. One must tear it off so that Destiny's solar truth will appear."[4] This is exactly what Yourcenar has done. Far from "investing incestuous love . . . with poetic charm and sentimental dignity,"[5] she narrates a story of passion that derives its power from the ineluctable force of fatality and a stark authorial objectivity. In her 1981 postface she explains why she chose this incestuous theme ("it has quickly become for the poets the symbol of all sexual passions all the more violent that they are more constrained, more punished, and more hidden" [*O*, 1030]), without moralizing, just as she refrained from judgment in her treatment of homosexuality in other works. Indeed, the father clearly accuses and resents Anna for Miguel's death, whereas their mother has always recommended that they must never hate each other and she may even have been suggesting that their love was not sinful: "Do not worry. All is well" (*O*, 866). Present again, as in Yourcenar's writings of the 1930s, is the close correspondence between love and sadism, desire and cruelty, pleasure and pain.

Unlike the first part of "D'après Rembrandt," the original story, which takes place in Holland only, "Un Homme obscur" describes the life of Nathanaël, the protagonist, in various lands. From Greenwich, England, where he was a teacher's assistant and read some of the classics, medieval tales, and "several plays of a certain Shakespeare,"[6] he sails on a ship bound for Jamaica, then to the northeast coast of America. After four hard years in the New World, during which he was married to Foy, a young consumptive girl, he only inchoately understands the world, almost in impressionistic fashion, as if his thought barely touched the surface of things.

Upon his arrival in Amsterdam, Nathanaël goes to work as proofreader in his Uncle Elie Adriansen's printing-publishing company. In his job he can continue his education by reading Greek and Roman texts, comparing their society to his and seeing the injustice of the present-day situation (religious, political, social, and economic). Whereas in the *Attelage* story he spent many of his free moments as an itinerant preacher, easily taken advantage of, who associated Christ not with God but with man and, therefore, "learned to see in every man a crucified carpenter" (*Mo,* 173), in the 1982 story he fully appreciates the grandeur of Christian principles but rejects as nonsense dogma and religion: "Nathanaël's mother lived and would die fortified by her Bible . . . but Foy had innocently lived and stopped living with no more religion than the grass and the source waters" (*O,* 929).

He falls in love with Saraï (a name meaning "mockery"), a Jewish honky-tonk singer and prostitute, whom he marries when she becomes pregnant. A few months later, however, she leaves him and moves back in with her mother in the Jewish ghetto where she gives birth to a son named Lazare. After an evening during which Nathanaël has unsuccessfully sought human warmth and companionship, he passes the night outside in the snow and, suffering from pleurisy, finds himself in a charity hospital. He then convalesces in a philanthropic family's home where he becomes a butler.[7] There, his master's learned friends enjoy conversing with this educated and well-traveled servant although they are not interested in his actual knowledge of and anecdotes about the American continent because these do not fit with their commonplace notions ("he tried in vain to convince them that Norumbega was only an imposture and that its forests had no gold other than that of autumn" [*O,* 956]) or because his listeners either exaggerate his adventures or, on the contrary, reduce everything to European scale as though the new and exciting exoticism of America were not enough or too much to be appreciated and accepted.

In the spring he is sent as game warden to his master's property in the Frisian Islands. On the ship he overhears that his wife has been hung for robbery and when he arrives at his destination, on the beach, he cries out her name many times and gets no answer, as he gets none when he next cries out God's name. Now all alone except for migratory birds, Nathanaël becomes "a thing among things" (O, 991), merging his naked body with the night, as Zeno had let the sea enter his own naked body after his walk on the dune (A, 268–69). The old Jewish philosopher, whose page proofs Nathanaël had corrected, wanted "to give chaos at least the appearance of an order" (O, 967) but Nathanaël knows now that God or the Self or Nothingness is not at the center of the universe, that ultimately all, including man, is guided by chance, and that he will die soon (at twenty-seven) like other creatures around him. As the surrounding omnipresent dawn slowly fades, "he rested his head on a grassy mound and settled himself in as if to sleep" (O, 1000).

Far from being the failure suggested by the modest anonymity of the title, the protagonist's life, thanks to his sensitivity, his love for plants, trees, birds, animals, his gentleness, his refusal to act according to preconceptions or judgmental ideas, can be considered successful, for Nathanaël has evolved the peace of mind and acceptance of cosmic darkness the other characters, rich burghers and poor workers alike, have been unable or unwilling to acquire.

The second part of the "Rembrandt" portrait tells of the young years of Lazare, the orphan son of Nathanaël and Saraï, who is raised by the Adriansens, discovers the theater, and subsequently departs with a troupe of Shakespearean actors. "Une Belle Matinée" relates in a few pages how Lazare, here raised by Saraï's mother, learns several parts of the English repertoire under the adept tutoring of an actor living at his grandmother's house, is hired to play Rosalind in As You Like It, packs his belongings, falls asleep, and dreams his future life: "Alternately girl and boy, young and old, murdered child and murdering brute, king and beggar, prince dressed in black and motley fool of the prince."[8] The theater is thus a store of illusions—reinforced by costumes, greasepaint, and hairpieces—where every player, like Proteus, takes on a thousand forms and where love, friendship, and good humor exist next to jealousy, hatred, and cruelty: in short, all the stage's a world. Lazare goes off with the troupe, and, after a heavy rain, the weather starts to clear. It is indeed going to be "a beautiful morning" as all the actors are looking forward to some good food and Lazare "to the great skirt with the silver gores."[9] The driver of the carriage, disguised as Death, appears again, but is greatly reduced in his symbolic significance: "Death drives the team, but so does life," concludes Yourcenar in her postface.[10]

"Une Belle Matinée" may appear to some readers as only an *ébauche,* a preliminary outline, yet it is this very unfinished sketchiness (suggested, too, by the "matinée" of the title) which parallels the hero's life, itself at its early beginning (he is twelve years old) and quite naturally only outlined as well, plus the sum of all human possibles present in Lazare's oneiric reality, that makes of this fine narrative a small gem.

Theater

Yourcenar's drama has received less acclaim from critics and public than her fictional creations, because, on the one hand, it is complex in its characters and themes and, on the other, it follows a rather traditional dramatic form. Collected into two volumes (*Théâtre,* 1971) her plays offer another dimension to her art and a more visual immediacy of her philosophical concerns and interpretation of the human condition and ethos.

Rendre à César (Render unto Caesar, 1961)[11] is an adaptation of her novel, *Denier du rêve.* Naturally, the action, plot developments, and relationships remain the same, as do most of the characters, although some have gained stature in their transfer and others have lost it. For example, Father Cicca has now become an important figure who delivers one of the key monologues of the tragedy: addressing himself, he questions his own ability to counsel and lead his self-involved parishioners and to share with them the joy of knowing God's goodness: "As long as there will be in the street an old and deaf woman, a blind beggar, . . . a donkey suppurating under its burden, a starving, wandering dog, make me not fall asleep in the sweetness of God"[12]—a prayer that will later appear in the Franciscan prior's own meditations on the misery of the world. In her Cornelian "History and Examination of a Play," Yourcenar explains that, in writing the 1934 novel, she wanted to use "a form, half-lyrical, half-narrative, open to all variety of facts and gestures but capable of also rendering faithfully the deep song of the characters and the muted oneiric and mythic accompaniment."[13] Less apparently oneiric and mythic, the play attempts to be more realistic but misses under its weight of interminable soliloquies and long-winded dialogues, which were either less numerous or less conspicuous in *A Coin in Nine Hands*. This may explain why it was never accepted for the stage.

Produced in English in 1942 at the Wadsworth Athenaeum of Hartford, Connecticut, *La Petite Sirène* is, in Yourcenar's generic description, a "divertissement dramatique"[14] based on *The Little Mermaid* by Hans Christian Andersen.

The sirens are symbolic of the whole sea, as they swim to submerged cities, sunken ships, and coral reefs and to the two poles in the benevolent company of whales. Ostracized from this group is the little mermaid who not only sings with human words but is tormented by her love for the Danish prince and dreams to be a woman who walks: "You are committing the supreme crime," admonishes the Water Witch, "you want to change elements, to change species" (*T*, 1:155), yet she grants her a human body in exchange for her voice. Although at first the young prince is attracted by her wondrous beauty, he quickly tires of her silence, pragmatically preferring the countless advantages of a marriage to the Norwegian princess, even if she is shrewish, unfeeling, and pedestrian. Egged on by her former sisters ("Kill! Kill! Kill! . . . He has betrayed you, . . . he has disdained you, . . . he has misunderstood you" [*T*, 1:170]), the little siren decides to stab the sleeping couple to death and with their blood she will be able to regain her mermaidenhood. However, she refuses to surrender to her hatred and pain, drops her knife, and stretches her arms out to the angel-birds: after she has given up water, she now gives up earth to go to air and "fly . . . beyond sea foam, beyond space!" (*T*, 1:171–72).

The language is highly poetic, as befits a fairy tale, and conveys in a sober tone the "passage from archeology to geology, from the meditation on man to the meditation on the earth,"[15] undergone by Yourcenar who in many respects is also a "sister of the seals, the flying fish and polar whales" (*T*, 1:171).[16]

A short one-act play, *Le Dialogue dans le marécage* (Dialogue in the marshland), first appeared in print in 1932 in *La Revue de France*. She writes in a note that the piece follows Japanese form and that its three main characters are modeled after *nō* protagonists (the obsessed pilgrim, his monk-acolyte, the sought-for phantom).[17]

Sire Laurent returns to the Sienese region after a twelve-year absence hoping to be forgiven by Pia, the adolescent wife he virtually imprisoned in a manor house lost amid foul-smelling noxious marshes. Such mistreatment, while done with the best of intentions ("to save her from her youth, I surrounded her with solitude" [*T*, 1:183]), could only drive her to sin and hence to more solitude. His aptly named companion, Brother Candide, tries to remonstrate with him regarding the wrongness of his misogyny and show him that women are the source of all love. Because Pia's death would be her revenge, Sire Laurent is relieved to find her alive and well and is even somewhat surprised to see her happy in her confinement, thus underlining her special saintliness. She is distraught, however, to learn from him that her lover, Simon, married, had children, and died in France—until she declares that, actually, he comes to visit her every month, or is it every week? Is her husband, then, lying to her? Is she delirious and self-deluding, as her two servants, Candide, and Sire Laurent are thinking? Is it simply that some new lover for her will always be Simon? Is Laurent in fact speaking with his wife or with a neighborwoman mistaken for Pia? Is he not himself crazed with guilt and despair, imagining that he is conversing with a ghost appeared through the miasmic gases of the swamps? These questions remain unanswered since Brother Candide takes him away forever and since Pia, not hearing what he wants to ask her, offers him a rose—a recurring image in the play (*T*, 1:185–86, 188, 192, 200–201)—that is the symbol of both love and evanescence, and as such of life itself.

Inspired by Euripides' interpretation of the murder of Aegisthus and Clytemnestra, *Electre ou la chute des masques* (Electra, or masks will fall), was staged at the Théâtre des Mathurins in 1954 where it failed due to the director's and actors' inability to express the frenetic cruelty of the play. Notwithstanding bad reviews, Gabriel Marcel remarks on its "great beauty"[18] and Thomas Mann writes glowingly that it is yet another proof of Yourcenar's considerable talent.[19] She wrote a new *Electre* in order to find out what would happen if the givens of the ancient Greek legend were changed and if, for instance, Orestes were not the legitimate son of Agamemnon but the *bastard child of Aegisthus:* regardless of one's filial status, the play shows "the horrible or sublime persistence of human beings in remaining themselves whatever happens. . . . Evidence has no hold on [them] because no certainty or disillusionment is stronger than

the mixture of instinct and will which makes them what they are"
(*T*, 2:20).

Electra has been nurturing the idea of the double murder for five
years and now that her brother has returned from exile with Pylades,
she will kill her mother and stepfather in an ambush. She refuses
to call her deed a matricide but rather an act of justice and vengeance
that will finally liberate her from all her rancor and hatred. Pylades
is the cynically cold realist who tries halfheartedly to convince her
not to proceed because in such circumstances the result brings neither relief nor solace: "One gets rid of the dead provided only that
one replaces them" (*T*, 2:41). The fragile and young Orestes, on
the other hand, refuses to commit the crime in a cowardly way but
would rather kill Clytemnestra as an anonymous woman, devoid of
her motherhood, lying in bed next to an equally anonymous assassin,
himself devoid of human characteristics. Electra (crossing herself)
insists that he participate in this ritual mass "in the name of the
Father . . . in the name of the Son," and the three accomplices,
reconciled to their joint action, recite a pagan Lord's Prayer: "Our
Father who art in the tomb . . . Thy will be done . . . Thy
vengeance come . . . And forgive us our trespasses . . . As we do
not forgive those who trespassed against you" (*T*, 2:47, 51).

In the meeting between mother and daughter, Clytemnestra gives
her explanations and justifications for Agamemnon's death, but as
Electra presents a defense of her father she inadvertently betrays her
voyeuristic behavior brought about by jealousy of her mother and
sexual hunger for Aegisthus. This truth is so hard to bear that in
a burst of irrational anger, to silence her mother, as much as to
mete out a just punishment, Electra strangles her. When Aegisthus
arrives, he resignedly accepts whatever bad end will befall him,
knowing full well that often "the innocent . . . appear to be mur-
derers" (*T*, 2:67).[20] But first he reveals that Pylades is the expedient
friend, a paid traitor/double agent, that through him Aegisthus
helped to support Orestes, and especially that *he*, the usurper and
tyrant, is Orestes' father. He was forced, therefore, to kill Agamemnon to protect his own son, for in another ironic misunderstanding, he feared Electra's denunciation of his affair. Orestes must
now choose which father he will hate more and, to escape the vicious
cycle that would forbid him to become himself, he stabs Aegisthus
unaided, preferring, according to Lothar Rubinstein, a return to
pre-Oedipian dependency on the mother to submission to a posses-

sive father who is also living and well.[21] Refusing to admit the futility of revenge, Electra, Orestes, and Pylades flee together while Aegisthus informs his guards that he was attacked by masked bandits and that these three wore no masks. In a final ironic twist, Electra's husband is arrested ("Someone must always take the rap" [*T*, 2:78]) and readily puts on the mask of the guilty: "You're right. . . . I know everything. . . . Nothing was done without me . . ." (*T*, 2:79).

Masks have fallen thanks to the revelations of the *deus ex machina* that is Aegisthus: the three acolytes have at last been able to accomplish their destiny as it has been spun for them since the day of Agamemnon's death eighteen years before. "The play's the thing / Wherein I'll catch the conscience of the King," hopes Hamlet, the Renaissance Orestes (act 2, scene 2), and indeed Yourcenar's characters refer several times to their acting in a drama (*T*, 2:62, 64, 66) for which they need to wear antique masks. When they take these off, instead of vulnerable faces, they expose their true heroic but frozen nature.[22]

Le Mystère d'Alceste (1963) dramatizes in the form of a medieval "Mystery Play of Alcestis" the fear of death and the miracle of resurrection by adapting the Greek myth (as arranged by Euripides) of a wife's supreme sacrifice on behalf of Admetus, the husband she loves. Even with all his power, the Sun is unable to save the young woman, forever fated to die, and no substitute volunteers for that honor. "A brute, perhaps, a naïf with a pure heart" (*T*, 2:111) could wrestle for Alcestis' soul.

Neighbors and servants gossip about their sundry activities and the goings-on in the house, while Alcestis bids farewell to her favorite simple things, resents having to die, and, to cover this resentment, quarrels with her husband about his flirtations and the probably brief period of his coming widowerhood; for his part, Admetus is shattered, and not a little guilty, at watching the ravages on her face, and he promises to write poetry that will immortalize her—adding in a most tactless manner that he will "look the lights of another world dawn in your eyes" (*T*, 2:118)—although he is unwilling to acknowledge that he would rather contemplate her dead, young, and beautiful than alive, old, and ugly.

After several interludes of atrocious comic relief (with such *fâcheux* as an unctuous funeral director, his unfeeling parents, a literal-minded mayor), Admetus allows Hercules to eat, bathe, and sleep

in his home but does not mention his wife's death. Hercules acts
in character when he speaks stupidly and insensitively, when he
gets completely drunk and lustful, when he quickly repents and
decides to set things right again, and when he knows that no one
can defeat him. He is, of course, the brute, the "naïf with the pure
heart" whose strength might conquer Death. In his subsequent
confrontation with Death, the hero is serially tempted into inaction,
glory, and ultimate knowledge. When he rejects Death's entice-
ments ("Your secrets are the only ones I'm sure to know one day")
and refuses to be taken in by sophistry and to be afraid, Death
admits, "I have no breathable air other than human terror" (*T,*
2:148), and releases Alcestis from his hold. At first, she does not
want to live again, objecting to having to return to Admetus and,
especially, to die again for him; she proposes instead to become
Hercules' travel companion, but he convinces her to keep on climbing back. During an exchange between Hercules and Admetus, the
defender of the weak and of just causes tests Admetus' fidelity by
presenting him a young woman whom he refuses with disgust; when
the widower realizes who it is, he is obviously overtaken with love
and tenderness. As Hercules leaves for the Caucasus, he has the last
all-too-human word: "And tell little Phyllis to be a little nicer next
time" (*T,* 2:161).

Yourcenar borrows from the Theseus story the plot of *Qui n'a pas
son Minotaure?* (Who does not have his Minotaur?, 1963) which she
calls a "sacred divertissement." Far from being a light comedy, the
play presents a world in which each participant must deal with his
own destiny, and the title itself suggests that all of us have a monster
to confront and maybe to vanquish.

The fourteen victims, sent to Crete in tribute to King Minos,
echo in their own way these multiple attitudes: the fatalism of one
is answered by the Epicureanism of another, existential bad faith is
corrected by acceptance of His love, the state's collective survival
is negated by individual suicide, stoicism and indifference are can-
celed by divine purpose ("There has to be a reason for so many
holocausts" [*T,* 2:187]). On this prison ship, which recalls the Nazi
death trains, Theseus too must come to understand the springs of
his being—a situation he does not enjoy because with free will come
action and accountability. Just as Theseus has doubts and conscience
pangs, Ariadne and Phaedra are also suffering from obscure desires
to be someone else or to escape elsewhere. "My sister aims to destroy

you," Ariadne tells the Greek prince, "it would please me to create you" (*T,* 2:204), and it is her mistake to trust him and to think him more than weak and cowardly.

In the Minotaur's cave, deep like "my inner darkness, . . . my entrails" (*T,* 2:207), Theseus meets with voices that rise from his memory and his potential and reveal the diverse aspects of his psyche, mind, fears and hopes, ambitions and lies. What evolves of this encounter with his unconscious is the image, not of the legendary hero born to greatness, but of a sordid opportunist, using his handsomeness to compensate for morality ("If I hadn't known how to handle women . . ." [*T,* 2:209]), plotting to have his father assassinated, abandoning Ariadne, killing his son Hippolytus, until, unable to view his true visage, he tries to destroy it: "I think I'm the one who dies" (*T,* 2:214). He is incapable of learning from the past, of understanding the present, and of drawing correct conclusions about the future. All that is left of his struggle with his Minotaur is the notion of more glory to come and a child's rusty sword.

Ariadne, who wanted a perfect Theseus, almost a god, is disappointed at discovering that he never killed the Cretan monster and that he never assumed his existence and his freedom. This is why, as he and Phaedra sail off to their true fate ("I hope, Theseus, I'll be able to make Hippolytus love me" [*T,* 2:231]), she willingly accepts to be abandoned on the island of Naxos where she meets a strange figure named "Bacchus (God)," who appears in several guises, including that of the Minotaur, to fulfill man's expectations of his other self ("man creates me in his own image" [*T,* 2:227]). Unable to answer her questions and doubts, he offers her a conscious immortality which emanates from letting herself go: "You are already dead, Ariadne. And this is precisely how your eternal life begins" (*T,* 2:229).

Played in 1980 at the Théâtre Marie-Stuart, *Qui n'a pas son Minotaure?* was panned by the critics and quickly closed. Jean Blot very perceptively attributes Yourcenar's theatrical failures to her revival of ancient times without the necessary modernization of characters and response to contemporary sensibility, as Giraudoux has done.[23] Gabriel Marcel, for his part, states that *Electre* and *Le Mystère d'Alceste* are worthy of the Comédie-Française repertory company where the acting and directing would surely bring out their poetic and dramatic qualities.[24]

Poetry

In addition, Yourcenar has also written three collections of poems—
two published in her late teens (and paid for by her father) and one
in 1956.

Le Jardin des chimères (The garden of chimaeras, 1921) is the
dramatic rendition of the story of Icarus who, "in love with the Sun
and wanting to escape the sadness of the wondrous Garden, succeeds
in taming the Chimaera and taking her wings to rise to the star."[25]
The legend is presented in two parts: the first one shows Icarus
eager, even anxious,

> Boire à ta source pure, ô froide Vérité!
> Voir Hélios, enfin! . . .
>
> To drink from your pure source, oh cold Truth!
> To see Helios at last! . . .
>
> (J, 28)

and arguing with Daedalus, his father, the tired and disillusioned
philosopher who tried in vain to find answers to his questions ("Et
jamais la Réponse en tous lieux demandée / Ne put me satisfaire
ou ne put me calmer" ["And never the Answer I everywhere re-
quested / Could either satisfy or becalm me," J, 35]) and who, now
completely resigned, is almost glad to die and enter night's darkness.
In the second part, the young adventurer, after his victory over the
Chimaera, flies high toward the sun "Pour que je sente, ô Roi, se
consumer mon âme / Dans ton brasier resplendissant" ("So I can
feel, oh my King, my soul consume itself / In your resplendent
fire," J, 73). Unmoved by the Sirens' calls of love, by the Winds'
promises of far-away lands, by Peoples' pledges of obedience and
glory, he refuses all human blandishments in the hope that he will
soon know "in a greedy moment / The kiss of eternity!" (J, 103).
That he fell to his death is not a failure since, as Helios exclaims
in the closing monologue, Icarus is glorious for having dreamed
and tried, regardless of his ultimate end:

> Gloire à celui qui veut s'évader du mensonge!
> Gloire à celui qui tente, en un suprême élan,
> De monter . . .
> Vers le rayonnement des clartés immortelles! . . .

> Le sacrifice obscur n'est jamais infertile. . . .
>
> Glory to him who wants to flee the lie!
> Glory to him who tries, in a supreme surge,
> To rise . . .
> Toward the radiance of the immortal gleam! . . .
> The obscure sacrifice is never infertile. . . .
>
> (*J*, 117)

This long poem, which one critic qualified at the time as being "very ambitious, very long, and very boring,"[26] already points to certain themes, for instance, the quest for the Absolute, that will recur in Yourcenar's later works. It does not, however, paint "the enormity, the excessiveness of human illusions and ambitions," as she declared in a 1968 magazine interview:[27] her statement is in obvious contradiction with the Sun's eulogistic praise and indicates more the ideas of the mature writer, which a Hadrian or Zeno could share, than those of a teenager.

Her next book of poetry appeared a year later bearing the weighty title of *Les Dieux ne sont pas morts* (The gods are not dead). The first poems ("Les Rafales," "Regrets helléniques," and "Le Palais du Passé")[28] emphasize her intense desire to escape from her corrupt modern society to the ideal world of Greek antiquity and of the East with its heroes, artists, myths, and gods, such as the powerful Astarte Syrica who recalls Baudelaire's Beauty:

> Sûre de ma beauté, je choisis pour miroir
> Mon bouclier, l'Orgueil, et le Désir, mon glaive . . .
> Des siècles de malheurs et de faste insensé
> Ont modelé mon âme impassible et cruelle . . .
> Je suis la Destructrice et l'Epouse stérile . . .
>
> Sure of my beauty, I choose for my mirror
> My shield, Pride, and Desire for my sword . . .
> Centuries of misfortunes and of insane splendor
> Have modeled my unperturbed and cruel soul . . .
> I am the Destroyer and the sterile Wife . . .
>
> ("Astarte Syrica")

or the maidenly Ariadne who accepts all forms of servitude and sacrifice to be loved by "the young man with the dark eyes" ("Paroles d'Ariane").

Many of the poems are grouped along inspirational themes: "Provençal Landscapes," "Byzantine Mosaics," "Songs," "Florentine Paintings." "Persian Embroideries" owes much to Victor Hugo, especially *Les Orientales*, for its subject matter and technique, from the exotic settings in which "Schéhérazade voit descendre / Le soir de la Millième Nuit . . ." ("Scheherazade sees the evening / Of the Thousandth Night fall . . ." ["Schéhérazade"]) to "Danseuse," whose very rhythm follows the dancer's fluid movements, to "Le Jardin d'Yblis" which, in spite of its great beauty, brings death and destruction.

In the untitled series, "Aphrodite Ourania" is the longest poem of the book and the most important example of the "deathlessness of the gods." Indeed, the goddess has all the powers since she has been incarnated in so many different forms, and this forever. As the august Virgin, she knows or governs all ("Je dirige d'en haut l'immuable harmonie / Des lignes, des parfums, des couleurs, des accords" ["I direct from on high the immutable harmony / Of lines, perfumes, colors, chords"]); unlike the earthly Aphrodite she is dressed in "unalterable azure" and is celebrated by the great Plato as *the* Muse; she was also Pallas and Victory for whom soldiers willingly died. As the celestial Aphrodite she gave "thought and love and life" to man; she is also the Virgin Mary ("Je tenais dans mes bras l'humanité meurtrie / Comme un enfant divin qu'allaitait mon amour" ["I held within my arms wounded humanity / Like a divine child drinking the milk of my love"]); today, she is called Science and reveals new knowledge and secrets to her disciples. And ultimately, she is "the divine Unity" in which she gathers all mankind.

Although André Fontainas called this 1922 collection the "grave and charming volume of a true poet,"[29] it did not receive much critical notice either, and Yourcenar felt later that "it would have been better to throw these two productions into the wastebasket" (*Y*, 53). More talented to write prose than poetry, she did not publish another work of poetry until *Les Charités d'Alcippe et autres poëmes* (*The Alms of Alcippe and Other Poems*) appeared in 1956. Unlike her previous poetic compositions, this series was well received, and Emilie Noulet's is quite typical of these favorable reviews: "*Les Charités d'Alcippe*, . . . besides its classical qualities, has this justness of tone, this plenitude of song, this rarity as well as this fitness of image which make great poetry."[30]

Alcippe the poet gladly gives first his heart to the Sirens, then his soul to the statues, and finally his body to the ghosts:

> Comme un nard répandu sur la gorge des Reines
> J'existe à tout jamais dans ce que j'ai donné.
>
> Like a nard on the breast of the Queens, I'm aware
> I exist for all time in the things that I gave.[31]

Many poems deal with varied topics such as death, fellow artists (for instance, Jean Cocteau and Marie Laurencin), famous sonneteers of the past or even the sonnet form itself ("Quatorze cygnes blancs ou quatorze colombes / Quatorze anges debout veillent sur le passé" ["A road of tombs we walk, where fourteen doves, / Fourteen white swans, or angels, guard our loves"], "Sonnets")—an image and an idea Yourcenar had already been struck with in a poem also titled "Sonnets" from *Les Dieux ne sont pas morts* ("Quatorze grains d'or flamboyant au soleil" ["Fourteen grains of gold blazing in the sun"]). Other poems have the body or love for their theme, like "Hospes Comesque" (this title comes from the second line of Hadrian's verse [*M, i*) or "Le Poëme du Joug" ("Poem of the Yoke"). A few pieces show Guillaume Apollinaire's influence, such as the *calligrammatique* "Poëme pour une poupée russe" ("Poem for a Russian Doll") with its interesting triangular typographical setup, while several have definite symbolist resonances, like the very Verlainean "Cantilène pour un joueur de flûte aveugle" ("Song for a Blind Flute Player"):

> Flûte dans la nuit solitaire,
> Présence liquide d'un pleur,
> Tous les silences de la terre
> Sont les pétales de ta fleur.
>
> Lonely flute that plays in the night,
> Liquid presence of a tear,
> All the silences on earth
> Like petals to your flower adhere.

In a letter dated 6 June 1963, Yourcenar writes that, even though her poetry is not really modern, she nonetheless thought all the more about the meaning of "these atoms, exploded or dissolved, this phantom form which is ceaselessly outlined and then comes undone before fixing itself, these thousand little waves of the ego springing and falling back on their spot in a vapor of foam, sometimes gay, sometimes aggressive and greedy, and always desperate. . . ."[32] It is unfortunate for us, therefore, that she has not written more of this highly personal poetry.

Translations

Besides her own numerous writings, Marguerite Yourcenar has often translated into French the works of others that might otherwise have remained unknown to and unappreciated by a reading public lacking linguistic knowledge or ability. These translations range from Virginia Woolf's *The Waves* (1937) and Henry James's *What Maisie Knew* (1947), both done for financial reasons, to Greek and Punjabi poetry.[33]

In his article,[33] Jean Darbelnet has convincingly demonstrated the excellence of her literary renditions, not only in her using the *mot juste* but also in giving the words' underlying connotations. Of the various examples taken from the Woolf and James fiction and from Hortense Flexner's poetry (1969) that he cites, the most interesting are: "the dark castle" becomes "la masse sombre du château," thereby giving the building a physical presence in the landscape; "the mind grows rings" is now "l'esprit s'élargit d'année en année comme le tronc d'un chêne," which implies both the growth and the power of the mind; "the apple tree stark, in the moonlight" is translated as "la dure silhouette du pommier au clair de lune"—a tree at once hard and hard to see. Jean-François Josselin agrees with Darbelnet and most other critics, praising "the dazzling translation" of *Ce que savait Maisie* and *Les Vagues*.[34]

The noted American poet and translator, Richard Howard, writes that "Yourcenar has translated [Constantin Cavafy's poems] into triumphant French prose,"[35] to which Maurice Lebel adds that "she makes one think of the admirable translator that was Jean Racine. This is saying it all."[36] Hélène Ioannidi, however, found several errors and misreadings in the French text, in spite of the close collaboration with Constantin Dimaras, director of the Sorbonne's Institut néo-hellénique, and the inclusion of an important series of notes explaining the many difficulties encountered by the two translators. Nevertheless, she recognizes that on the whole the 1958 work is of high quality.[37]

Yourcenar's next translation, *Fleuve profond, sombre rivière* (Wide, deep, troubled water, 1966) is a fascinating anthology of Negro spirituals that takes its title from the first verse of one of the songs. Dating her strong interest back to her visit to South Carolina in 1937, Yourcenar collected poems along thematic lines (for instance, slavery, the two Testaments, Apocalypse, and lullabies) which all seem to emphasize in the most visceral fashion mankind's universal response to utter misery, suffering, hope, and joy. These spirituals, which she justly compares to the German *lieder* of the minnesinger and the poems of twelfth-century Italian mystics,[38] were translated into "a popular language . . . that would give the immediate impression of having come from the people" (*Y*, 204):

> J'vais déposer mon bouclier et mon épée
>> Au bord d'la rivière . . .
> J'vais plus m'exercer pour la guerre. . . .
>> ("I Ain't Goingt' Study War No More")

> J'ai une belle robe, t'as une belle robe,
> Les enfants d'Dieu ont tous une robe. . . .
>> ("All God's Chillun Got Wings")

> Montez dans l'train les p'tits enfants,
> Ya d'la place dans l'compartiment!
>> ("Git on Board, Little Chillen")

> Quéqu'fois, j'me sens comme un enfant sans mère
>> Loin d'la maison,
> Tout seul, tout sombre, avec ma peine amère,
>> En toute saison. . . .
>> ("Sometimes I Feel Like a Motherless Child")

> Personne ne sait l'chagrin qu'j'ai eu,
> Personne ne l'sait, sauf que Jésus,
> Personne ne sait l'chagrin qu'j'ai eu,
>> Ah, ah, Alléluia!
>> ("Nobody Knows De Trouble I've Seen")

> Descends, Moïse, au bord de la rivière,
> Dis au vieux roi que not' peuple s'en va. . . .
>> ("Go Down, Moses")[39]

La Couronne et la lyre (The crown and the lyre, 1979) is Yourcenar's translation of ancient Greek poetry, spanning about twelve centuries, or from the first Parthenon to St. Sophia's. Of the some hundred and ten poets represented, the collection includes of course such greats as Homer, Anacreon, Pindar, Callimachus, and Sappho, as well as many anonymous or lesser-known contributors.

Far from being a work for the specialist or erudite scholar, however, her book appeals to the average reader (and its fourteen weeks on the best-seller list in France confirm this), because it not only offers him a pure aesthetic pleasure but also an essential understanding of himself as he is torn, like his Greek brothers, between "the passionate lust for life and the bitter questioning of life."[40] She has chosen examples from the many kinds of poetic expression in order to present the full range of emotions and experiences, from the simple ("Cléotas dort ici. Pleure sur son tombeau, / Voyageur. Il mourut tout jeune; il était beau") to the lyrical ("Et l'aube a réveillé le bruyant rossignol") to the misanthropic ("Je suis mort sans laisser de fils, et regrettant / Que mon père avant moi n'en eût pas fait autant").[41] By her selection of authors and poems, Yourcenar illustrates again her love for an antiquity that is close both to the Ideal and to the human condition.[42] And, although her harshest critic, George Steiner, qualified her language as bland and uniform, pallid and mundane, monotonous and dated, most others, like Jean Guitton and Jean Pollack, admired her beautiful French and prosody.[43]

Finally, in 1983, Marguerite Yourcenar translated black gospels which she then recorded for Disques Auvidis, a French company: on one side, Marion Williams sings and, on the other, Yourcenar recites the French text. (These poetic renditions of black American lyrics appeared in 1984 with the title *Blues et gospels.*) She also translated for the June issue of *La Nouvelle Revue française* several poems by Amrita Pritam, a contemporary Punjabi writer. Later that year, Gallimard published to critical acclaim her translations of James Baldwin's *The Amen Corner* and five nō plays by Yukio Mishima.

Essays

Yourcenar has written nonfiction prose as well, which covers a whole range of subjects, reflecting her broad intellectual curiosity, interest, and erudition. This includes a fascinating preface to the translation of Prince Felix Yousoupoff's *La Fin de Raspoutine* (1964).

Most of her essays, though, are literary introductions to her translations or dissertations prefacing her own creative works. Her only full-fledged studies are on the Greek poet Pindar, published at the beginning of her career, and on Yukio Mishima, the modern Japanese novelist, in 1980.

Pindare (1932), which Yourcenar considers a bad piece of work written much too young and mainly out of financial need (*Y,* 38, 64), is part biography, part cultural history, part literary presentation. The biographical chapters relate not only the known facts about the fifth-century B.C. lyric poet, his education and musical training, his discovery of nature's beauties and promises, his idealization of homosexual love, his knowledge of ancient myths and folklore, his travels through Greece and Sicily, his conservative thinking tempered by empirical moderation, but also supposes and imagines plausible facts about his life, his thought, his parents, his ascendants: "The mother . . . was probably very young, already fat and very submissive. . . . As for the father, it suits us to picture him as one of these . . . thrifty and wealthy aristocrats. . . . [His ancestors,] the Aegeidae, had helped the sons of Herakles in their conquest of the Peloponnese" (*P,* 23, 33). This fanciful re-creation of what might have been done and said, the legends and oracles surrounding Pindar's birth and youth, "the vast swirls of races" (*P,* 155) will become, as we have seen in chapter 5, an important philosophical and literary device used in the writing of her autobiography. Moreover, she brings to life a whole period of history, its battles, intrigues, weaknesses, pleasures, grandeur, leaders, poets and philosophers, and sportsmen, too, since virile beauty and athletic prowess were as much admired and richly compensated then as in our own culture today. In fact, Pindar wrote many of his best odes in praise of victors in the stadium or at the Games. Using daring images and metaphors, in addition to a poetry extolling victories and patriotic feelings and the great and mythic deeds of gods, kings, and famous men, for which he was well paid, this poet laureate also composed poems about love, despair, and the bittersweet realization that man is ephemeral, no more than "the dream of a shadow."[44] Much as she will later find beauty in Negro spirituals, gospels, and blues, Yourcenar knows intuitively that Pindar's "songs represent the individual soul's moment returned to the human community" (*P,* 18) and, therefore, have a power that is universal and atemporal: "We are concerned with the same problems, we are subject to the same dreams. . . . The human spirit, on the same road, continually encounters the same phantoms" (*P,* 183).

Originally published in 1962, *Sous bénéfice d'inventaire* (Without preconceptions) is composed of seven essays (the piece on Selma Lagerlöf was added for the 1978 edition) written for various literary reviews or as prefaces to an artist's complete works.

The first article deals with the *Historia Augusta* and contends that it is difficult for any student of history to fully believe accounts of the past, mainly because what appears authentic and plausible has often been filtered and interpreted through "the mores, prejudices, and ignorance of each epoch."[45] And yet the work of these six Roman historians is still moving in its poetic force and, in spite of obvious biases, useful as object lessons that can equally be applied to medieval emperors, Hitler, Mussolini, or contemporary leaders: "The modern reader is at home in the *Historia Augusta*" (*So,* 27). The next essay, on *Les Tragiques,* while showing the defects of Agrippa d'Aubigné's epic, assesses it as a great religious act of witnessing full of mysticism and relived anger. It also reminds us that the Renaissance was an age of religious turmoil and intolerance, of political unrest and inhuman conduct as well, and that the poem's lack of success may have been due to the fact that "nothing . . . becomes more quickly outmoded than martyrs" (*So,* 143).

"Ah, mon beau château"—the title comes from a children's round—is a meditation worthy of a Balzac plot on the castle of Chenonceaux and the devouring power of money. She traces the succession of owners, from a rich bourgeois' widow named Catherine Bohier to Diane de Poitiers who received it in gift from Henri II, from Queen Catherine de' Medici to Louise de Lorraine to Gabrielle d'Estrées. The Condé family, in need of quick money, sold it to Mme Dupin (hostess of Jean-Jacques Rousseau), and it later became the property of a certain Mme Pelouze, the sister of President Jules Grévy's dishonest son-in-law. Ingeborg M. Kohn argues that the very title points out joy and pain ("Ah")—gala affairs and costume balls and sadness and loneliness—plus the ambiguous motif of ownership (*"mon* [my] beau château").[46] In the end, Yourcenar distances herself from "these too well-known figures . . . of French history or of French literary history" (*So,* 88) to introduce the backstage workers of this beautiful house (servants, cooks, valets, scullery maids within, gardeners, masons, game wardens, farmers, architects without), along with the birds and the animals of the forest, the trees, the river waters "which for centuries have been washing history's old cast-offs" (*So,* 89). She has thus gone from the human to the universal and from the temporal to the eternal.[47]

Slightly misquoting the line from Victor Hugo's "Les Mages,"[48] Yourcenar analyzes next Giambattista Piranesi's darkly fantastic world of *Imaginary Prisons,* with its ever-present niches, pulleys, staircases, wheels, torture instruments, chains, and labyrinthine corridors which dwarf a heretofore egocentric man well placed at the center of the universe to the rank of homunculus. While the somberness of Piranesi's etchings may have been caused by malaria attacks, the obvious claustrophobia and agoraphobia of the *Carceri,* devoid as they are of air and natural life, have demonic characteristics especially evident in the world of dreams: "the negation of time, the displacing of space, the suggested levitation, the intoxication of the impossible reconciled or overcome, a terror . . . close to ecstasy, . . . the absence of a visible link or contact between the parts or the characters of the dream, and finally the fatal and necessary beauty" (*So,* 112). Furthermore, Yourcenar interprets these masterpieces as representative of the Italian baroque conception of the Last Judgment, Hell and *Dies Irae* in which the world is a gigantic prison and man the Lilliputian prisoner.

In "Ah, mon beau château," she achieved a certain *compartmentalization of time* (her phrase; *So,* 46–47) and, in "Le Cerveau noir de Piranèse" (The dark brain of Piranesi), the spatialization of time wherein present, past, and future are forever fixed in the engraver's nightmarish visions—an idea she had already alluded to thirty years before: "There is neither past nor future, but only a series of successive presents."[49] Both essays, though, as Jacques de Ricaumont indicates, are less concerned with "the creation of beauty than the exploration of the human unconscious."[50]

Selma Lagerlöf, the late Swedish novelist and Nobel laureate, is one of the few women writers Yourcenar considers a genius. Preferring the "epic tales" (from the title; *So,* 131) to the novels, she admires the diamondlike quality of the style, the bigger-than-life characters, the omnipresent beauty of nature, the elemental conflict between pagan and Christian, and the prelapsarian innocence of animals.

André Gide made the following entry in his 1940 *Journal:* "I was reading yesterday the amazing article by Marguerite Yourcenar on the amazing poet Cavafy. . . ."[51] Her essay is indeed one of the most insightful studies of the Greek poet from Alexandria, Egypt. Despite his birth, life, and death in this cosmopolitan Middle Eastern city, Cavafy is not interested in Oriental landscapes, and his realistic descriptions of city streets and cafés are presented only in relation to human events. He belongs to Greater Greece and finds in its past and legends the sources of his inspiration for the historical poems. Although the homosexual love poems are free of the stigma of sin, if not of the fear of scandal, it was not until his old age that Cavafy accepted a happiness defined by "ancient hedonism . . . without abjection, without rhetoric, without . . . this frenzy for interpretation [and by] a kind of pure and simple assertion of all sensual freedom" (*So,* 179). After Yourcenar has delineated these two thematic categories, she convincingly proves that all the poems are in fact historical in nature (*So,* 181) and then she demonstrates how the *self* appears everywhere—and this is the reason why she can now posit "that in the last resort there are in him only personal poems" (*So,* 196).

The last essay of the *Inventaire* collection, "Humanisme et hermétisme chez Thomas Mann," shows that Mann's highly complex novels are to be interpreted as the quest for humanistic knowledge and, ultimately, wisdom itself. Death, however, is often either the only escape from or punishment for "the original sin of intelligence" (*So,* 205). Citing many examples of occult/religious/magic themes, such as initiation, eroticism, dreams, incest, music, and *nigredo* accompanied or not by death (*So,* 216–23), she places this very German "analyst of mutations and passage" in the tradition of the known alchemists and hermetists and of their fellow travelers like Goethe and Mozart. Moreover, she sees in his works a corroboration of her own theories about space and the historical moment which is part of an infinite continuum she explicitly associates with "a cosmic notion of eternity" (*So,* 201).

Mishima ou la vision du Vide (Mishima, or the vision of the void, 1980) examines the fiction of the Japanese author and views his death by hara-kiri on 25 November 1970 as an act of dignity and lucidity. Taking a strong stance in her critical approach ("let us always remember that the central reality is to be sought in the work"),[52] Yourcenar puts Yukio Mishima's novels in the context of his cultural environment, part Japanese, part European, part American. She explains how he felt the unbearable nausea of a people torn from its ancestral roots and how deeply he regretted the Japan of the samurai and its chivalric ideals, the speculations of Buddhist thought, and the beauty of silk prints. But, and without apparent contradiction, she also underscores the traumatic influence of several childhood memories on both his life and his works. In a few perspicacious pages, she analyzes Mishima's early novels and plays and devotes—rightfully so—half of her monograph to *The Sea of Fertility* (1968–70). This series of four novels depicts the disintegration of Japanese society from 1912 to 1970, or from the aftermath of the victories in the Pacific (1905) to the political and military troubles of the 1920s and 1930s, to the crushing defeat of World War II and American occupation to the robotization of man, and finally to the octogenarian Honda's discovery of the great Void.

Yourcenar is fascinated by Mishima's aesthetic and ritualized suicide committed at the optimal moment and she refers to it as a masterpiece,[53] to the tetralogy as a testament,[54] and to all his writings as the principal explanation of such a violent and premeditated end.

Yourcenar's other essays, some published in the late 1920s, deal with a variety of topics, from political science to the arts and from history to philosophy. In all, she shows the same incisive mind and felicity of style already evident in her other creative endeavors, and these essays have helped not only to form her intellectual baggage (for instance, the pieces on Boecklin, Mozart, and the making of a saint) but also to shape her *Weltanschauung* (the role of the merchant in civilization, a fatally sick but beautiful Europe [in 1929], man's relation to the natural world of plants, animals, and stones). Her observations on different religious philosophies (Zen Buddhism, Bede the Venerable, Greek mythology, *Gita Govinda*) and her literary commentaries (including on how she gets inspiration and chooses her subjects for study or fiction) further elucidate our understanding of her thought. Many of these essays were collected and released at the end of 1983 under the title, *Le Temps, ce grand sculpteur* (Time the great sculptor).[55]

Of a different but related genre is *Les Yeux ouverts* (With open eyes, 1980), a series of impromptu interviews done over several years, and often quoted here, in which Yourcenar discusses all manner of subjects with, in Pierre de Boisdeffre's words, "a stunning loftiness, authority, and freedom of expression."[56]

Chapter Seven
Conclusion

Marguerite Yourcenar, by the very independence and creativity of her production, is one of the most original writers of the second half of the twentieth century, and throughout the world today, from the United States to Japan, from Finland to Israel, her enthusiasts are legion.

Her literature portrays characters who rebel against arbitrary moral and sexual strictures ("I believe in the nobility of refusal")[1] and underscores male homosexuality and deviance as important themes common to many of these characters, along with a certain sadistic comportment in their relationships with their feminine counterparts. This is why Yourcenar has been accused by critics, if not of advocating misogyny, at least of favoring contempt for women, citing the conspicuous absence of heroines as proof of their conclusions. Not only are such statements unfair, they are also incorrect. Female characters do appear in her fiction and theater and either have an important supporting role (for instance, Thérèse of *La Nouvelle Eurydice*, Plotina of *Mémoires d'Hadrien*, Martha of *L'Oeuvre au noir*) or are essential to the action of the story and the psychology of the participants: these include, for example, Marcella *(Denier du rêve)*, Sophie *(Le Coup de grâce)*, Electra *(Electre)*, Anna *(Anna, soror . . .)*, and many from *Nouvelles orientales* and *Feux*. What has vexed some of her detractors has been Yourcenar's unwillingness to join the needless discrimination inherent in the category, *women* writers, since she feels that she does not write as a woman and sees no difference between feminine and masculine writing.[2] Rather, she is an author who happens to be a woman and whose works should be judged on their merit alone. That she objects to a new ghettoization has not precluded her from committing her energy and talent to good causes, including equality—but not similarity—of women in personal, political, or professional endeavors, the fight for Indian and black rights (see her preface to *Fleuve profond, sombre rivière*) and against other social and governmental evils *(Y, 275–91)*.

By demonstrating that the power of myth and the ineluctable course of history are useful sources of inspiration, Yourcenar has achieved her creative goals. Moreover, she has constructed an absurd world in which man's destiny is directed as much by chance *(le hasard)* as by free will. Alexis, Conrad, Hadrian, Zeno, and the others share the undercurrents created by the conflicts between society's demands and their passions. If and how they resolve these intense inner struggles are, of course, in a large measure results of the strength of their personality. Although some flounder in an unsatisfactory limbo, the majority succeed in imposing their own view of the world, whether through conscious *open-eyed* acceptance of their selves or planned deliberate suicide.

Yourcenar's novels, plays, and essays reveal an artistic subtlety that makes evident the universality of her personages as well as their uniqueness, and it is to all these parallel qualities that readers and critics alike have been attracted. Because she has kept aloof of the literary problems and fashions of the post–World War II period, preferring a restrained, well-ordered classical form of narration to convey her protagonists' emotions and intellectual force, her influence is not immediately noticeable, and yet there seems to be on the part of several contemporary French authors a desire to emulate the coldly fiery style, the eternal drama of "the human adventure" *(So,* 31), the concerns about a universe on the verge of self-destruction found in her writings. This is especially evident of such new-generation novelists as François Fontaine (*L'Usurpation ou le roman de Marc Aurèle,* 1979), Serge Bramly (*La Danse du loup,* 1982), and Paul Tabet (*Elissa Rhaïs,* 1982). Outside France, the best-known example is Umberto Eco with his *The Name of the Rose* (1980): we find here a narrative technique and an authorial approach and method reminiscent of Yourcenar's great fictional masterpieces.[3]

Now in her eighties, Marguerite Yourcenar vigorously continues to write several books at once, in particular, the third volume of her autobiography and a collection of travel essays/memoirs under the tentative title borrowed from a phrase of Zeno's, *Le Tour de ma prison* (The round of my prison). We her admirers await their forthcoming publication with eager impatience.

Notes and References

Preface

    1. *Pindare* (Paris, 1932), 138; hereafter cited in the text as *P*.
    2. Interview with Jean Montalbetti, *Le Figaro,* 26 November 1977, 19.

Chapter One

    1. Much of this information is found in *Archives du Nord* (Paris, 1977); hereafter cited in the text as *AN*.
    2. Much of this information is found in *Souvenirs pieux* (Paris, 1974); hereafter cited in the text as *SP*.
    3. "Autobiographical Sketch," in *World Authors 1950–1970,* ed. John Wakeman (New York, 1975), 1586.
    4. In *Les Yeux ouverts: Entretiens avec Matthieu Galey* (Paris, 1980), she tells her interviewer that she had read Aristophanes' *The Birds* and Racine's *Phèdre* at age eight or nine (28); hereafter *Les Yeux ouverts* cited in the text as *Y*.
    5. Jean d'Ormesson says that her adopted name sounds vaguely Turkish: see his *Réponse au Discours de réception de Marguerite Yourcenar* (Paris, 1981), 62.
    6. Interview with Paul Guth, *Le Figaro littéraire,* 3 October 1959, 8.
    7. Interview with Jacques Chancel, Radioscopie (France Inter/Radio France), 11 June 1979.
    8. "Autobiographical Sketch," 1586.
    9. Preface to *Fires,* trans. Dori Katz in collaboration with the author (New York, 1981), ix; hereafter cited in the text as *F*.
    10. "Un Homme obscur," in *Comme l'eau qui coule* in *Oeuvres romanesques* (Paris, 1982), 909; hereafter *Oeuvres* cited in the text as *O*.
    11. "Reflections on the Composition of *Memoirs of Hadrian,*" in *Memoirs of Hadrian,* trans. Grace Frick in collaboration with the author (New York, 1963), 326; hereafter *Memoirs* cited in the text as *M*.
    12. *Washington Post,* 7 October 1983, sec. A, p. 34, col. 5.

Chapter Two

    1. Preface to *Alexis,* trans. Walter Kaiser in collaboration with the author (New York, 1984), xi; hereafter cited in the text as *Al*.

2. In an interesting critique of François Mauriac, Jean-Paul Sartre accuses the author of *La Fin de la nuit* of just such untoward manipulation: "M. François Mauriac et la liberté," in *Situations* (Paris: Gallimard, 1947), 1:36–57.

3. "J'étais habitué à envelopper les femmes de tous les préjugés du respect; je les haïssais dès qu'elles n'en étaient plus dignes" (*Alexis,* in *Oeuvres,* 25).

4. "Je me croyais le droit . . . de ne pas repousser l'unique chance de salut que me donnait la vie, . . . je comprenais que seul je ne guérirais plus. A cette époque, je voulais guérir" (ibid., 60).

5. Maurice Delcroix, "*Alexis ou le traité du vain combat:* Un Roman épistolaire de Marguerite Yourcenar," *Cahiers de l'Association internationale des Etudes françaises* 29 (1977):235.

6. Jean Blot, *Marguerite Yourcenar* (Paris, 1980), 103.

7. In *Les Yeux ouverts,* she declares, "I felt very close to Rilke during this period" (67). Numerous examples from the Rilke masterpiece indicate this connection; for instance: "I observed all these things with attention, and it occurred to me that this must be the place that had been destined for me; for I now believed I had at last arrived. Yes, fate goes wonderful ways"; "Fate loves to invent patterns and designs. Its difficulty lies in complexity. But life itself is difficult because of its simplicity"; and "We discover, indeed, that we do not know our part, we look for a mirror, we want to rub off the make-up and remove the counterfeit and be real" (Rainer Maria Rilke, *The Notebooks of Malte Laurids Brigge,* trans. M. B. Norton [New York: Norton, 1949], 57, 176, 194).

8. It would be wrong to imply, however, as Jacques Brenner does, that Yourcenar even used Gide's marital situation for her plot: see *Histoire de la littérature française de 1940 à nos jours* (Paris, 1978), 241.

9. Edmond Jaloux, review of *Alexis, Les Nouvelles littéraires,* 26 April 1930, 3. Yourcenar dedicated *Denier du rêve* to Jaloux.

10. This is somewhat reminiscent of the Gidean definition of a literary work: "A book is tight, full, smooth as an egg. One couldn't get anything else into it, not so much as a pinpoint, except by force, and its form would be smashed into pieces" (*Marshlands,* trans. George D. Painter [New York: New Directions, 1953], 43).

11. Patrick de Rosbo, *Entretiens radiophoniques avec Marguerite Yourcenar* (Paris, 1972), 18.

12. Pierre Audiat's review (*Revue de France,* July 1931, 141–44) is typical of the generally negative reception of *La Nouvelle Eurydice;* for a favorable critique, see Edmond Jaloux, *Les Nouvelles littéraires,* 13 February 1932, 3.

13. *La Nouvelle Eurydice* (Paris, 1931), 13; hereafter cited in the text as *N.*

14. Blot, *Yourcenar*, 105.

15. Afterword to *A Coin in Nine Hands*, trans. Dori Katz in collaboration with the author (New York, 1982), 169; hereafter cited in the text as *C*.

16. In the "Histoire et Examen d'une pièce" prefacing her *Rendre à César* (Paris, 1971), Yourcenar mentions that the action goes from around noon on 20 April 1933 to about 6:00 A.M. on 21 April (1:25).

17. C. Frederick Farrell, Jr., and Edith R. Farrell discuss in their perceptive article "Mirrors and Masks in Marguerite Yourcenar's *Denier du rêve*," *Papers in Language and Literature* 17 (1981):307–19, the theme of duality and duplicity so prevalent among the characters; reprinted in their *Marguerite Yourcenar in Counterpoint* (Lanham, Md., 1983), 29–44.

18. In an earlier passage, her husband had already compared her to Medusa (*A Coin*, 82).

19. There is also an ironic deflation here, similar to that found in Stendhal and Proust, of the empty cockalorum well hidden behind a bemedaled uniform.

20. The "état civil" appended to *Rendre à César* indicates the protagonists' birth and death places and dates. Most interesting are those for Alessandro Sarte who was among the three hundred and thirty-five Italian patriots massacred by Kesselring's S.S. on 24 March 1944 in the Ardeatine quarry, for Oreste Marinunzi who fell at Stalingrad on 30 October 1943, and for Massimo Iacovleff who died at Auschwitz on 1 May 1945 (1:133–34).

21. "C'est priser sa vie justement ce qu'elle est, de l'abandonner pour un songe," Michel de Montaigne, "De la diversion," *Essais*, bk. 3, chap. 4, in *Oeuvres complètes* (Paris: Gallimard, 1962), 817.

22. Another story, "Les Emmurés du Kremlin," was removed from the final version "comme décidément trop mal venu" (postscript to *Nouvelles orientales*, in *Oeuvres romanesques*, 1215).

23. Rosbo, *Entretiens*, 153.

24. André Guyaux, "Le Lait de la mère," *Critique* 35 (1979):371: review of *Nouvelles orientales*.

25. Blot, *Yourcenar*, 87.

26. *Coup de Grâce*, trans. Grace Frick in collaboration with the author (New York, 1957), 29; hereafter cited in the text as *CG*.

27. Henri Hell, "Une Tragédie racinienne," *Cahiers des Saisons* 38 (1964):293.

28. John Charpentier, review of *Le Coup de grâce*, *Mercure de France*, 1 October 1939, 382.

29. In two contradictory scenes, Sophie refuses in one all feminine "accomplices" to seduction (*Coup*, 36) and in the other she overdoes the "whorish" look (ibid., 59).

30. Rosbo, *Entretiens*, 81.

31. "L'homme se ment toujours, consciemment et inconsciemment. Il organise son dialogue avec lui-même comme son dialogue avec autrui, derrière les barrages de la logique intérieure" (interview with Claude Mettra, *Les Nouvelles littéraires*, 27 June 1968, 3).

Chapter Three

1. Yourcenar indicated in an interview that she had been encouraged by Jules Romains to resume work on Hadrian's story: see *Les Nouvelles littéraires*, 22 May 1952, 6.

2. Emile Henriot, *Le Monde*, 9 January 1952, 7; Robert Kemp, *Les Nouvelles littéraires*, 10 January 1952, 2; Gérard d'Houville, *La Revue des Deux Mondes*, 15 February 1952, 736; and André Thérive, *Ecrits de Paris*, January 1952, 113.

3. Thomas Mann, *Letters*, trans. and ed. Richard and Clara Winston (New York, 1971), 660, and *Mythology and Humanism: The Correspondence of Thomas Mann and Karl Kerényi*, trans. Alexander Gelley (Ithaca, N.Y., 1975), 205.

4. The name derives solely from the fact that the Fémina jury is composed totally of women; prizes are awarded to men and women novelists alike.

5. The title of this first part comes from a poem by Hadrian given in the epigraph and is translated on the last page of the novel (*Memoirs*, 295).

6. Rosbo, *Entretiens*, 87.

7. As early as 1922, Yourcenar had been struck by the physical beauty and inner purity of "Antinoos aux jardins de Tibur": see her poem, "L'Apparition," in *Les Dieux ne sont pas morts* (Paris, 1922), 71. Philippe-Joseph Salazar notes that this part could easily be read separately as an erotic novella whose themes would be Hadrian's political acumen and spiritual strength, plus an appeal for compassion: "Sur *Mémoires d'Hadrien:* L'Idéal narratif," *French Studies in Southern Africa* 10 (1981):65.

8. In *Feux* (1936), Yourcenar had already written: "Je ne me tuerai pas. On oublie si vite les morts" (*Oeuvres romanesques*, 1135).

9. Rosbo, *Entretiens*, 65.

10. Janet Whatley, "*Mémoires d'Hadrien:* A Manual for Princes," *University of Toronto Quarterly* 50 (1980–81):225. She calls Hadrian's decision his "first gift . . . to the Empire."

11. Jacques Vier, "L'Empereur Hadrien vu par Marguerite Yourcenar," *Etudes littéraires* 12 (1979):29–30.

12. Jacques Brosse, "La Présence du passé," *Cahiers des Saisons* 38 (1964):296.

13. Interview in *U.S. News and World Report*, 28 July 1980, 61.

14. See, for instance, such popularizing texts as Jacques Bersani et al., *La Littérature en France depuis 1945* (Paris, 1980), 309, 867; Pierre de Boisdeffre, ed., *Dictionnaire de la littérature contemporaine* (Paris, 1963), 685; Germaine Brée, *Littérature française: Le XXᵉ Siècle 1920-1970*, ed. Claude Pichois (Paris, 1978), 364; Gaëtan Picon, *Panorama de la nouvelle littérature française* (Paris, 1976), 147.

15. Rosbo, *Entretiens,* 47.

16. Ibid., 48.

17. For a detailed bibliography consulted for the composition of the novel, see her "Bibliographical Note" at the end of *Memoirs,* 299–314.

18. Roland Barthes arrived at a similar conclusion in his essay, "Le Discours de l'Histoire," *Information sur les sciences sociales,* August 1967, 72–74.

19. Paul Valéry, *Regards sur le monde actuel,* in *Oeuvres* (Paris: Gallimard, 1960), 2:935.

20. Robert Champigny, "Histoire et roman," *L'Esprit créateur* 7 (1967):99.

21. Blot, *Yourcenar,* 123.

22. "Ah, mon beau château," in *Sous bénéfice d'inventaire* (Paris, 1962), 22–24.

23. A. A. Mendilow, *Time and the Novel* (London: Nevill, 1952), 106.

24. Blot, *Yourcenar,* 121.

25. Rosbo, *Entretiens,* 61.

26. Gérard Genette, *Figures* (Paris: Le Seuil, 1972), 3:105.

27. Avrom Fleishman, *The English Historical Novel* (Baltimore: Johns Hopkins University Press, 1971), 14.

28. Rosbo, *Entretiens,* 52–53.

29. Marcel Proust, *A la recherche du temps perdu* (Paris: Gallimard, 1954), 1:452.

30. *L'Ecrivain devant l'Histoire* (Paris, 1954), 16.

31. Answers to "Le Questionnaire Proust," *Livres de France,* May 1964, 11, 13.

32. Arnold Toynbee, *Civilization on Trial* (Cleveland: World Publishing Co., 1958), 19.

33. Jean Ballard, review of *Mémoires d'Hadrien, Cahiers du Sud* 34 (1951):493.

Chapter Four

1. *The Abyss,* trans. Grace Frick in collaboration with the author (New York, 1976), 189; hereafter cited in the text as *A.*

2. Theophrastus Paracelsus, in *Unpartheyische Kirchen und Ketzerhistorie,* ed. Gottfried Arnold (Frankfurt am Main, 1700–1715), 2:432; cited

in Ronald D. Gray, *Goethe the Alchemist* (Cambridge: Cambridge University Press, 1952), 31.

3. "D'après Dürer," in *La Mort conduit l'attelage* (Paris, 1934), 15; hereafter *La Mort* cited in the text as *Mo*. The expression is used again in *The Abyss*, 10.

4. In *Les Yeux ouverts*, Yourcenar erroneously gives 27 February as Zeno's birth date (191).

5. A similar anecdote is told about Admiral de Coligny's wife: "Ces trois sepmaines sont achevées." See Agrippa d'Aubigné, *Histoire universelle*, ed. Alphonse de Ruble (Paris: Laurens, 1887), 2:13.

6. For the sources used for this novel, see *The Abyss*, 361–74.

7. His scientific and philosophical inquiries also resemble those of the pre-Socratic philosopher, Empedocles: see Yourcenar, "Empédocle d'Agrigente," *Revue générale*, January 1970, 31–36.

8. Blot, *Yourcenar*, 136. Instead, according to a letter of 20 July 1969 to Léonie Siret, an admiring reader, and published in *La Nouvelle Revue française* (1 April 1980), Yourcenar declares that the first draft of her work, begun in her early twenties, was entitled *Remous* (183).

9. Gaston Bachelard, *La Psychanalyse du feu* (Paris: Gallimard, 1938), 22.

10. In a short essay, "L'Improvisation sur Innsbruck," Yourcenar writes: "Par un mouvement naturel qui n'a rien que de bon, de rassurant aussi, on se détache de tout ce qu'on a connu, de tout ce qu'on a possédé" (*Revue européenne*, December 1930, 1025).

11. Calling mirrored truth a "lure," Karlis Racevskis suggests that "the Self is . . . a mirage and its relation to the world in which it sees itself reflected is constantly undermined by uncertainty" (*Michel Foucault and the Subversion of Intellect* [Ithaca, N.Y.: Cornell University Press, 1983], 34).

12. Emese Soos, "The Only Motion Is Returning: The Metaphor of Alchemy in Mallet-Joris and Yourcenar," *French Forum* 4 (1979):10.

13. Michel Aubrion, "Marguerite Yourcenar ou la mesure de l'homme," *Revue générale*, January 1970, 21.

14. C. G. Jung, whom Yourcenar read for her background research (see *The Abyss*, 366), draws parallels between the prime matter essential in alchemy and the components of human personality as well as between the omnipotent fire and man's intense will to consciousness: see *Collected Works*, vol. 12, *Psychology and Alchemy*, trans. R. F. C. Hull (Princeton: Princeton University Press, 1974), 412–14 and passim.

15. Maurice Delcroix, "Marguerite Yourcenar entre le Oui et le Non," *Marche romane* 31 (1981):74.

16. Interview with Jean Chalon, *Le Figaro littéraire*, 18 June 1971, 28.

17. Rosbo, *Entretiens*, 133.

18. Geneviève Spencer-Noël notes that these constant juxtapositions of opposites are an important part of the alchemical process and that, naturally, Yourcenar would use them in her novel: see *Zénon ou le thème de l'alchimie dans "L'Oeuvre au noir" de Marguerite Yourcenar* (Paris, 1981), 42.

19. In a radio interview, Marguerite Yourcenar declared to Jacques Chancel that Zeno wants to die comfortably (Radioscopie, 11 June 1979) and to Matthieu Galey that she "loved him too much . . . to make him suffer too much" (*Les Yeux ouverts*, 188).

20. Mircea Eliade, *Forgerons et alchimistes* (Paris: Flammarion, 1977), 130.

21. The photograph of the manuscript's title page by Gisèle Freund is included among the illustrations preceding page 33 of *Les Yeux ouverts*.

22. Yourcenar employs the masculine word "compagnon" to emphasize the quasi-hermaphroditic qualities of the sensual and tender *dame de Frösö* who represents for Zeno the erotic incarnation of Good.

23. Laure Jordan, "La Peste et sa représentation: Peinture, littérature et cinéma" (Ph.D. diss., Ecole des Hautes Etudes en Sciences Sociales, Paris, 1983), 91.

24. Yourcenar appended her close translation of Campanella's trial proceedings (1597–1601) to her discussion of "Ton et langage dans le roman historique," *La Nouvelle Revue française*, October 1972, 120–23; reprinted in *Le Temps, ce grand sculpteur* (Paris, 1983), 52–58.

25. "Ton et langage," 105; reprinted in *Le Temps*, 36.

26. Interview with Jean Prasteau, *Le Figaro littéraire*, 2 December 1968, 20.

27. Jean Onimus, *La Table ronde*, November 1968, 223; Sophie Deroisin, *Revue générale belge*, June 1968, 124; Gonzague Truc, *Ecrits de Paris*, October 1968, 29; Gennie Luccioni, *Esprit*, December 1968, 782–83; Henri Clouard, *La Revue des Deux Mondes*, July–August 1968, 424; Robert Kanters, *Le Figaro littéraire*, 17 June 1968, 19, and *Revue de Paris*, August–September 1968, 121.

28. Rosbo, *Entretiens*, 137, n. 1.

Chapter Five

1. The title of her autobiography comes from a seventeenth-century text by a religious philosopher, Jan Amos Comenius (Komenský), adapted into French by Michel de Crayencour, Yourcenar's father: *Le Labyrinthe du Monde et le Paradis du Coeur* (Lille: Danel, 1906).

2. That the author felt obliged to mention why she included *Feux* in *Oeuvres romanesques* would indicate that this work is not easily classifiable: see her foreword in *Oeuvres romanesques*, ix. Moreover, in all the Yourcenar

works published in the "Collection Blanche," Gallimard lists *Feux* under the rubric "Poèmes et Poèmes en prose."

3. C. Frederick Farrell, Jr., and Edith R. Farrell, "Marguerite Yourcenar's *Feux:* Structure and Meaning," *Kentucky Romance Quarterly* 29 (1982):27; reprinted in their *Marguerite Yourcenar in Counterpoint,* 51.

4. The use of the indicative mood "ressemblait" rather than the more doubtful subjunctive underlines further the certainty of the likeness of the two figures.

5. Rosbo, *Entretiens,* 150.

6. Preface to *Feux* (Paris, 1957), 3.

7. Introductory notice to *Feux* (Paris, 1936), 9.

8. "Autobiographical Sketch," 1586. In a letter to Yvon Bernier dated 4 January 1978, she states that her work was "indépendante des concepts freudiens de l'époque" (quoted in Bernier, "Itinéraire d'une oeuvre," *Etudes littéraires* 12 [1979]:8).

9. Preface to *Les Songes et les sorts* (Paris, 1938), 25: "Ce n'est pas dans ce dessein que je les [ces textes] ai réunis, non plus que dans le dessein contraire." Hereafter *Les Songes* is cited in the text as *S.*

10. "Les seuls profonds exégètes que ce sentiment [l'amour] ait sus-cités jusqu'ici sont l'orgue et le violoncelle" (ibid., 10).

11. Blot, *Yourcenar,* 160.

12. Gaston Bachelard, in his beautifully poetic *L'Eau et les rêves* (Paris: Corti, 1942), writes that "un instant de rêve contient une âme entière" (71), and Yourcenar herself declares in *L'Oeuvre au noir:* "Ces catégories fantômales [du rêve] ressemblaient fort à ce que les hermétistes prétendaient savoir de l'existence d'outre-tombe, comme si le monde de la mort eût continué pour l'âme le monde de la nuit" (*Oeuvres,* 794).

13. Michel Foucault, *L'Ordre du discours* (Paris: Gallimard, 1971), 29–30.

14. Philippe Lejeune, *L'Autobiograpie en France* (Paris: Le Seuil, 1971), 19.

15. Roy Pascal, *Design and Truth in Autobiography* (Cambridge, Mass.: Harvard University Press, 1960), 11; Louis A. Renza, "The Veto of Imagination: A Theory of Autobiography," *New Literary History* 9 (1977):3; James Olney, *Metaphors of the Self: The Meaning of Autobiography* (Princeton: Princeton University Press, 1972), 42, 332; Philippe Lejeune, *Le Pacte autobiographique* (Paris: Le Seuil, 1975), 14; and Jean Starobinski, "Le Style de l'autobiographie," *Poétique* 3 (1970):257.

16. *Théâtre* (Paris, 1971), 2:167.

17. Georges Gusdorf, *La Découverte de soi* (Paris: Presses Universitaires de France, 1948), 469.

18. It is interesting that Simone de Beauvoir has expressed the same desire in her Preface to *La Force de l'âge:* "J'ai consenti, dans ce livre, à

des omissions, jamais à des mensonges" ([Paris: Gallimard, 1960], 11, n. 1).

19. Interview with Mattieu Galey, *Réalités,* October 1974, 72.

20. Rosbo, *Entretiens,* 67.

21. Ibid., 50.

22. Georges Gusdorf, "Conditions et limites de l'autobiographie," in *Formen der Selbstdarstellung: Analekten zu einer Geschichte der Selbstportraits,* ed. Günther Reichenkron and Erich Haase (Berlin: Duncker and Humblot, 1956), 109.

23. Interview with Jacques Chancel, Radioscopie, 11 June 1979.

24. "La forme entiere de l'humaine condition," Michel de Montaigne, "Du repentir," *Essais,* bk. 3, chap. 2, in *Oeuvres complètes* (Paris: Gallimard, 1962), 782.

25. *Réalités* interview, 72.

26. *La Couronne et la lyre* (Paris, 1979), 382.

Chapter Six

1. A short story, "Le Premier Soir," published in 1929 (*La Revue de France,* 435–49) under Yourcenar's name, was in fact written mainly by her father: see the chronology in her *Oeuvres romanesques,* xvii.

2. Postface to "Un Homme obscur," in *Comme l'eau qui coule* (in *Oeuvres romanesques,* 1032).

3. In "D'après Greco," Anna whispers, "Mi bien amado" (*La Mort conduit l'attelage* [Paris, 1934], 170): the shorter phrase found in the 1981 version makes her dying words less literary, hence more spontaneous and stronger.

4. Blot, *Yourcenar,* 68.

5. Mario Praz, *The Romantic Agony,* trans. Angus Davidson (New York: Oxford University Press, 1970), 111.

6. "Un Homme obscur" (in *Oeuvres,* 904–5).

7. In the initial story, Nathanaël is discovered almost frozen dead in a doorway; he dies several days later in an Amsterdam hospice.

8. Postface to "Une Belle Matinée," in *Comme l'eau qui coule* (*Oeuvres,* 1038).

9. "Une Belle Matinée" (ibid., 1021).

10. Postface to "Une Belle Matinée" (ibid., 1038). In the 1934 text, she writes: "On avait chargé la Mort dont le drap blanc ne craignait rien, de diriger l'attelage de sorte que cette charrette de Thespis, comme la barque de Caron, semblait porter des ombres" (239). Such an image comes from Cervantes (postface, 1038) and perhaps also from a bas-relief, titled *Theatrica,* found in the Duomo Museum in Florence, Italy.

11. The title comes, of course, from Mark 12:17. Marcella pronounces the sentence when she "pays" for the gun to be used to assassinate Mussolini (*Denier du rêve*, 110, and *Rendre à César*, act 2, scene 2).

12. *Rendre à César*, in *Théâtre* (Paris, 1971), 1:58; hereafter *Théâtre* cited in the text as *T*.

13. "Histoire et Examen d'une pièce," in ibid., 1:13.

14. *La Petite Sirène*, in ibid., 1:135.

15. "A propos d'un divertissement et en hommage à un magicien," in ibid, 1:146.

16. In a letter published in *Le Monde* (2–3 March 1969) she condemns the wanton slaughter of baby seals out of greed, indifference, or vanity (12), adding in an editorial column in *Le Figaro* (16 February 1972): "Tout acte de cruauté subi par des milliers de créatures vivantes est un crime contre l'humanité qu'il endurcit et brutalise un peu plus" (1); reprinted in *Le Temps*, 194.

17. Note to *Le Dialogue dans le marécage*, in *Théâtre*, 1:176.

18. Gabriel Marcel, "Le Théâtre de Marguerite Yourcenar," *Livres de France*, May 1964, 6.

19. "Les gens disent qu'avec Hadrien vous avez réalisé votre destin, écrit le livre de votre vie et qu'après il n'y aura plus rien. . . . Les idiots! Quand on a écrit un tel livre, cela prouve au contraire qu'on a des capacités dont on peut attendre mieux encore et votre *Electre* est venue!" (Thomas Mann to Yourcenar; quoted in Ghislain de Diesbach, "La chose du monde la moins partagée," *Cahiers des Saisons* 38 [1964]:286).

20. In a similar thought, Sire Laurent says, "Les coupables sont les seuls qui s'imaginent être innocents . . ." (*Théâtre*, 1:200).

21. Lothar Henry Rubinstein, "Les Oresties dans la littérature avant et après Freud," in *Entretiens sur l'art et la psychanalyse*, ed. André Berge et al. (The Hague: Mouton, 1968), 236.

22. Blot, *Yourcenar*, 70.

23. Ibid., 60.

24. Marcel, "Le Théâtre," 7.

25. Prologue to *Le Jardin des chimères* (Paris, 1921), 11; herafter cited in the text as *J*.

26. Jean-Louis Vaudoyer, review of *Le Jardin des chimères*, *La Revue hebdomadaire*, 8 April 1922, 647.

27. Interview with Josane Duranteau, *Les Lettres françaises*, 27 November 1968, 20.

28. *Les Dieux ne sont pas morts* (Paris, 1922).

29. André Fontainas, review of *Les Dieux ne sont pas morts*, *Mercure de France*, 1 May 1923, 750.

30. Emilie Noulet, review of *Les Charités d'Alcippe*, *Synthèses*, October 1957, 97.

31. *Les Charités d'Alcippe et autres poëmes* (Liège, 1956), 12; *The Alms of Alcippe*, trans. Edith R. Farrell (New York, 1982), 13.

32. Yourcenar to Alain Bosquet, 6 June 1963; quoted in *Marginales* 24 (1969):85.

33. Jean Darbelnet, "Marguerite Yourcenar et la traduction littéraire," *Etudes littéraires* 12 (1979):51–63.

34. Jean-François Josselin, *Le Nouvel Observateur*, 25 February 1980, 64.

35. Richard Howard, "Yourcenar," *Vogue*, May 1981, 328.

36. Maurice Lebel, "Marguerite Yourcenar traductrice de la poésie grecque," *Etudes littéraires* 12 (1979):78.

37. Hélène Ioannidi, "Le Travail du poète et le problème de la traduction," *Critique* 299 (1972):364–68: review article of *Présentation critique de Constantin Cavafy*. In a published letter dated September 1963, Yourcenar explains her translating method, especially of poetry, as consisting in "giving a French equivalent of the original poem, in disembodying it so to speak, in order to reembody it in another language and as one may imagine the poet would have written it, had he written in French," quoted by Etienne Coche de la Ferté, "Madame Yourcenar et les scrupules du poète" (*Cahiers des Saisons* 38 [1964]:302).

38. Interview in *Réalités*, October 1974, 74.

39. *Fleuve profond, sombre rivière* (Paris, 1966), 137, 151–52, 156, 158, 94.

40. Preface to *La Couronne et la lyre*, 11.

41. Ibid., 93, 105, 309.

42. My review first appeared in *World Literature Today* 54, no. 3 (Summer 1980):472.

43. George Steiner, *Times Literary Supplement*, 4 April 1980, 391; Jean Guitton, *Le Monde*, 11 January 1980, 15; and Jean Pollack, ibid., 15, 22.

44. Pindar, *Pythian* 8, lines 95–96.

45. *Sous bénéfice d'inventaire* (Paris, 1978), 9; hereafter cited in the text as *So*.

46. Ingeborg M. Kohn, "The Castle and the Prison: Verbal Architecture of the Imaginary," paper read at the MLA Convention, New York, 28 December 1981.

47. Rosbo, *Entretiens*, 164.

48. "Le noir cerveau de Piranèse / Est une béante fournaise" (Victor Hugo, *Les Contemplations*, in *Oeuvres poétiques* [Paris: Gallimard, 1967], 2:784).

49. "Sixtine," *Revue bleue* 69 (1931):634; reprinted in *Le Temps*, 21.

50. Jacques de Ricaumont, "Inventaire," *Cahiers des Saisons* 38 (1964):297.

51. André Gide, *Journal* (Paris, 1954), 2:54.

52. *Mishima ou la vision du Vide* (Paris, 1980), 12.

53. Ibid., 13.

54. Ibid., 48.

55. This is the title of an essay discussing the creative artistry of time on architecture and sculpture, often turning these works into beautiful abstract forms (*Revue des voyages* 15 [1954]:6–9; reprinted in *Le Temps*, 59–66).

56. Pierre de Boisdeffre, review of *Les Yeux ouverts*, *La Revue des Deux Mondes*, January 1981, 174.

Chapter Seven

1. Interview with Françoise Mallet-Joris, *Le Nouvel Observateur*, 2 December 1968, 44.

2. Interview with Jacques Chancel, Radioscopie, 13 June 1979.

3. See Eco's *Postscript to "The Name of the Rose"*—itself a Yourcenarian device—trans. William Weaver (San Diego, Calif.: Harcourt, Brace & Jovanovich, 1984), 1–84.

Selected Bibliography

PRIMARY SOURCES

1. Prose Fiction

Alexis ou le traité du vain combat. Paris: Au Sans Pareil, 1929; with preface added, Paris: Plon, 1952; revised and definitive edition, Paris: Plon, 1965; Paris: Gallimard, 1971 (copyright holder).

La Nouvelle Eurydice. Paris: Grasset, 1931.

La Mort conduit l'attelage. Paris: Grasset, 1934.

Denier du rêve. Paris: Grasset, 1934; revised, enlarged, and with preface added, Paris: Plon, 1959; Paris: Gallimard, 1971 (copyright holder).

Nouvelles orientales. Paris: Gallimard, 1938; revised and with preface added, 1963; enlarged and definitive edition, 1978.

Le Coup de grâce. Paris: Gallimard, 1939; with preface added, 1966.

Mémoires d'Hadrien. Paris: Plon, 1951; with "Carnets de notes des *Mémoires d'Hadrien,*" Paris: Plon, 1958; Gallimard, 1971 and 1974 (copyright holder).

L'Oeuvre au noir. Paris: Gallimard, 1968.

Comme l'eau qui coule. Paris: Gallimard, 1982.

Oeuvres romanesques. Paris: Gallimard, 1982. This is the edition used for this study.

2. Nonfiction Prose

Pindare. Paris: Grasset, 1932.

Les Songes et les sorts. Paris: Grasset, 1938.

L'Ecrivain devant l'Histoire. Paris: Centre national de documentation pédagogique, 1954.

Sous bénéfice d'inventaire. Paris: Gallimard, 1962; enlarged and definitive edition, 1978.

Le Labyrinthe du Monde. 2 vols. Paris: Gallimard, 1974–77. Volumes entitled *Souvenirs pieux* and *Archives du Nord.*

Mishima ou la vision du Vide. Paris: Gallimard, 1980.

Les Yeux ouverts: Entretiens avec Matthieu Galey. Paris: Le Centurion, 1980.

Discours de réception à l'Académie française. Paris: Gallimard, 1981.

Le Temps, ce grand sculpteur. Paris: Gallimard, 1983.

3. Theater

Electre ou la chute des masques. Paris: Plon, 1954.

111

Le Mystère d'Alceste and *Qui n'a pas son Minotaure?* Paris: Plon, 1963.
Théâtre. 2 vols. Paris: Gallimard, 1971. This is the edition used for this
study.

4. Poetry
Le Jardin des chimères. Paris: Perrin, 1921.
Les Dieux ne sont pas morts. Paris: Chiberre, 1922.
Feux. Paris: Grasset, 1936; with a different preface, Paris: Plon, 1957;
revised, Paris: Plon, 1968; Gallimard, 1974 (copyright holder). De-
spite its "prose poems" label, it is included in *Oeuvres romanesques:*
this is the edition used in this study.
Les Charités d'Alcippe et autres poëmes. Liège: La Flûte enchantée, 1956.

5. Translations into French
Baldwin, James. *Le Coin des "Amen."* Paris: Gallimard, 1983.
Blues et gospels. Paris: Gallimard, 1984.
Cavafy, Constantin. *Poèmes.* In collaboration with Constantin Dimaras.
Paris: Gallimard, 1958.
Fleuve profond, sombre rivière. Paris: Gallimard, 1964.
Flexner, Hortense. *Poèmes.* Paris: Gallimard, 1969.
James, Henry. *Ce que savait Maisie.* Paris: Laffont, 1947.
La Couronne et la lyre. Paris: Gallimard, 1979.
Mishima, Yukio. *Cinq Nô modernes.* In collaboration with Jun Shiragi.
Paris: Gallimard, 1983.
Woolf, Virginia. *Les Vagues.* Paris: Stock, 1937.

6. Interviews

a. Books
Rosbo, Patrick de. *Entretiens radiophoniques avec Marguerite Yourcenar.* Paris:
Mercure de France, 1972.
Wakeman, John, ed. *World Authors 1950–1970.* New York: H. W.
Wilson, 1975. Includes "Autobiographical Sketch."

b. Newspapers and Periodicals
Les Nouvelles littéraires, 22 May 1952, 6.
Le Figaro littéraire, 3 October 1959, 8.
"Le Questionnaire Proust." *Livres de France,* May 1964, 11–13.
Les Nouvelles littéraires, 27 June 1968, 3.
Les Lettres françaises, 27 November 1968, 20.
Le Figaro littéraire, 2 December 1968, 20–21.
Le Nouvel Observateur, 2 December 1968, 44–45.
Le Figaro littéraire, 18 June 1971, 28.
Réalités, October 1974, 70–75.

Le Figaro, 26 November 1977, 19.
U.S. News and World Report, 28 July 1980, 61.

c. Radio
Chancel, Jacques. Radioscopie. France Inter/Radio France, 11–15 June 1979.

7. Editorials and Published Letters
"Letter to Alain Bosquet," 6 June 1963. In *Marginales* 24 (1969):85–86.
"Letter to Etienne Coche de la Ferté," September 1963. In "Madame Yourcenar et les scrupules du poète." *Cahiers des Saisons* 38 (1964):302.
"Letter." *Le Monde,* 2–3 March 1969, 12.
"Letters to Léonie Siret," 20 July 1969 and 17 January 1971. In *La Nouvelle Revue française,* 1 April 1980, 181–91.
"Une Civilisation à cloisons étanches." *Le Figaro,* 16 February 1972, 1. Editorial. Reprinted in *Le Temps, ce grand sculpteur,* 191–95. Paris: Gallimard, 1983.
"Letter to Yvon Bernier," 4 January 1978. In "Itinéraire d'une oeuvre." *Etudes littéraires* 12 (1979):8.

8. Translations into English
Memoirs of Hadrian. Translated by Grace Frick in collaboration with the author. New York: Farrar, Straus & Giroux, 1954; with "Reflections on the Composition of *Memoirs of Hadrian.*" New York: Farrar, Straus & Giroux, 1963.
Coup de Grâce. Translated by Grace Frick in collaboration with the author. New York: Farrar, Straus & Giroux, 1957.
The Abyss. Translated by Grace Frick in collaboration with the author. New York: Farrar, Straus & Giroux, 1976.
Fires. Translated by Dori Katz in collaboration with the author. New York: Farrar, Straus & Giroux, 1981.
The Alms of Alcippe. Translated by Edith R. Farrell. New York: Targ Editions, 1982.
A Coin in Nine Hands. Translated by Dori Katz in collaboration with the author. New York: Farrar, Straus & Giroux, 1982.
Alexis. Translated by Walter Kaiser in collaboration with the author. New York: Farrar, Straus & Giroux, 1984.
Plays. Translated by Dori Katz in collaboration with the author. New York: Performing Arts Journal Publications, 1984.
With Open Eyes. Translated by Arthur Goldhammer. Boston: Beacon Press, 1984.
The Dark Brain of Piranesi and Other Essays. Translated by Richard Howard in collaboration with the author. New York: Farrar, Straus & Giroux, 1984.

SECONDARY SOURCES

1. Literary Histories
Bersani, Jacques et al. *La Littérature en France depuis 1945.* Paris: Bordas, 1980.
Boisdeffre, Pierre de, ed. *Dictionnaire de la littérature contemporaine.* Paris: Editions universitaires, 1963.
Brée, Germaine, *Littérature française: Le XXᵉ Siècle 1920–1970.* Edited by Claude Pichois. Paris: Arthaud, 1978.
Brenner, Jacques. *Histoire de la littérature française de 1940 à nos jours.* Paris: Fayard, 1978.
Picon, Gaëtan. *Panorama de la nouvelle littérature française.* Paris: Gallimard, 1976.

2. Books
Blot, Jean. *Marguerite Yourcenar.* Paris: Seghers, 1971. 2d ed., 1980. A good introduction to Yourcenar despite overemphasis on the homosexual and sadistic currents of her works. Several derogatory passages were eliminated in the 1980 updated edition.
Farrell, C. Frederick, Jr., and **Edith R. Farrell.** *Marguerite Yourcenar in Counterpoint.* Lanham, Md.: University Press of America, 1983. A stimulating and perceptive collection of reprinted articles and papers dealing with specific aspects of her works.
Ormesson, Jean d'. *Réponse au Discours de réception de Marguerite Yourcenar.* Paris: Gallimard, 1981. A sketchy survey of her literary career and main lines by an ardent admirer and supporter.
Spencer-Noël, Geneviève. *Zénon ou le thème de l'alchimie dans "L'Oeuvre au noir" de Marguerite Yourcenar.* Paris: Nizet, 1981. A thorough presentation of alchemical notions and symbols in the 1968 novel. Also includes notes and commentaries on Michel Butor's *Portrait de l'artiste en jeune singe,* on the Jewish Cabbalah, and on C. G. Jung.

3. Articles
Aubrion, Michel. "Marguerite Yourcenar ou la mesure de l'homme." *Revue générale,* January 1970, 15–29. A provocative essay dealing with free will and fatality in Yourcenar's works.
Brosse, Jacques. "La Présence du passé." *Cahiers des Saisons* 38 (1964):295–97.
Darbelnet, Jean. "Marguerite Yourcenar et la traduction littéraire." *Etudes littéraires* 12 (1979):51–63. An excellent article on her translations from the English.

Delcroix, Maurice. *"Alexis ou le traité du vain combat:* Un Roman épistolaire de Marguerite Yourcenar." *Cahiers de l'Association internationale des Etudes françaises* 29 (1977):223–41. A well-argued stylistic interpretation of her first novel.

————. "Marguerite Yourcenar entre le Oui et le Non." *Marche romane* 31 (1981):72–80. Thoughtful treatment of Zeno's quest for truth.

Farrell, C. Frederick, Jr., and Farrell, Edith R. "Mirrors and Masks in Marguerite Yourcenar's *Denier du rêve.*" *Papers on Language and Literature* 17 (1981):307–19. A very good study of the theme of duality and duplicity prevalent among the characters of this novel.

————. "Marguerite Yourcenar's *Feux:* Structure and Meaning." *Kentucky Romance Quarterly* 29 (1982):25–35. A subtle analysis of the autonomous yet interdependent structure of this complex work.

Hell, Henri. "Une Tragédie racinienne." *Cahiers des Saisons* 38 (1964):293–95.

Horn, Pierre L. "Marguerite Yourcenar's *Le Labyrinthe du Monde:* A Modern Anti-Autobiography." In *The Writer and the Past,* edited by Donald L. Jennermann, 1–9. Terre Haute, Ind.: Indiana State University Press, 1981. Shows the originality of Yourcenar's two-volume autobiography.

Howard, Richard. "Yourcenar." *Vogue,* May 1981, 280–81, 328. Short overview of her work.

Jordan, Laure. "La Peste et sa représentation: Peinture, littérature et cinéma." Ph.D. diss., Ecole des Hautes Etudes en Sciences Sociales, Paris, 1983. An interesting discussion of the theme of the plague in, among others, *L'Oeuvre au noir.*

Kohn, Ingeborg M. "The Castle and the Prison: Verbal Architecture of the Imaginary." Paper read at the MLA Convention, New York. 28 December 1981. Forcefully demonstrates how Yourcenar tries to impose order on space.

Lebel, Maurice. "Marguerite Yourcenar traductrice de la poésie grecque." *Etudes littéraires* 12 (1979):65–78. A fine presentation of her translating talents.

Marcel, Gabriel. "Le Théâtre de Marguerite Yourcenar." *Livres de France,* May 1964, 4–7. Brief but insightful explanation of her theatrical failures.

Ricaumont, Jacques de. "Inventaire." *Cahiers des Saisons* 38 (1964):297–301. An intelligent piece on Yourcenar's essays and short stories.

Rubinstein, Lothar Henry. "Les Oresties dans la littérature avant et après Freud." In *Entretiens sur l'art et la psychanalyse,* edited by André Berge et al., 224–38. The Hague: Mouton, 1968. A psychoanalytical study of the Greek myth, as illustrated, for one, in Yourcenar's *Electre ou la chute des masques.*

Salazar, Philippe-Joseph. "Sur *Mémoires d'Hadrien:* L'Idéal narratif." *French Studies in Southern Africa* 10 (1981):57–67. Semiotic examination of the novel.

Soos, Emese. "The Only Motion Is Returning: The Metaphor of Alchemy in Mallet-Joris and Yourcenar." *French Forum* 4 (1979):3–16. A thought-provoking comparison between *Le Jeu du souterrain* and *L'Oeuvre au noir.*

Vier, Jacques. "L'Empereur Hadrien vu par Marguerite Yourcenar." *Etudes littéraires* 12 (1979):29–35.

Whatley, Janet. "*Mémoires d'Hadrien:* A Manual for Princes." *University of Toronto Quarterly* 50 (1980–81):221–37. A cogent and perceptive essay on the novel's political science themes.

4. Reviews

Audiat, Pierre. Review of *La Nouvelle Eurydice. La Revue de France,* July 1931, 141–44.

Ballard, Jean. Review of *Mémoires d'Hadrien. Cahiers du Sud* 34 (1951):493–97.

Boisdeffre, Pierre de. Review of *Les Yeux ouverts. La Revue des Deux Mondes,* January 1981, 174–75.

Canby, Vincent. Movie review of *Coup de Grâce,* directed by Volker Schlöndorff. *New York Times,* 6 February 1978, sec. 3, p. 15, col. 5.

Charpentier, John. Review of *Le Coup de grâce. Mercure de France,* 1 October 1939, 381–82.

Clouard, Henri. Review of *L'Oeuvre au noir. La Revue des Deux Mondes,* July–August 1968, 422–24.

Deroisin, Sophie. Review of *L'Oeuvre au noir. Revue générale belge,* June 1968, 124–25.

Fontainas, André. Review of *Les Dieux ne sont pas morts. Mercure de France,* 1 May 1923, 749–50.

Guitton, Jean. Review of *La Couronne et la lyre. Le Monde,* 11 January 1980, 15.

Guyaux, André. "Le Lait de la mère." *Critique* 35 (1979):368–74. Review of *Nouvelles orientales.*

Henriot, Emile. Review of *Mémoires d'Hadrien. Le Monde,* 9 January 1952, 7.

Horn, Pierre L. Review of *La Couronne et la lyre. World Literature Today* 54, no. 3 (Summer 1980):472.

Houville, Gérard d'. Review of *Mémoires d'Hadrien. La Revue des Deux Mondes,* 15 February 1952, 736–38.

Ioannidi, Hélène. "Le Travail du poète et le problème de la traduction." *Critique* 299 (1972):354–68. Review of *Présentation critique de Constantin Cavafy.*

Jaloux, Edmond. Review of *Alexis. Les Nouvelles littéraires,* 26 April 1930, 3.

————. Review of *La Nouvelle Eurydice*. *Les Nouvelles littéraires,* 13 February 1932, 3.

Kanters, Robert. Reviews of *L'Oeuvre au noir*. *Le Figaro littéraire,* 14 June 1968, 19–20; *Revue de Paris,* August–September 1968, 120–23.

Kemp, Robert. Review of *L'Oeuvre au noir*. *Les Nouvelles littéraires,* 10 January 1952, 2.

Luccioni, Gennie. Review of *L'Oeuvre au noir*. *Esprit,* December 1968, 782–83.

Noulet, Emilie. Review of *Les Charités d'Alcippe*. *Synthèses,* October 1957, 96–98.

Onimus, Jean. Review of *L'Oeuvre au noir*. *La Table ronde,* November 1968, 222–24.

Pollack, Jean. Review of *La Couronne et la lyre*. *Le Monde,* 11 January 1980, 15, 22.

Steiner, George. Review of *La Couronne et la lyre*. *Times Literary Supplement,* 4 April 1980, 391.

Thérive, André. Review of *Mémoires d'Hadrien*. *Ecrits de Paris,* January 1952, 112–17.

Truc, Gonzague. Review of *L'Oeuvre au noir*. *Ecrits de Paris,* October 1968, 29–30.

Vaudoyer, Jean-Louis. Review of *Le Jardin des chimères*. *La Revue hebdomadaire,* 8 April 1922, 647.

5. Miscellaneous

Diesbach, Ghislain de. "La Chose du monde la moins partagée." *Cahiers des Saisons* 38 (1964):286. Prints a letter from Thomas Mann to Yourcenar.

Gide, André. *Journal*. Vol. 2. Paris: Gallimard, 1954.

Mann, Thomas. *Letters*. Translated and edited by Richard and Clara Winston. New York: Knopf, 1971.

————. *Mythology and Humanism: The Correspondence of Thomas Mann and Karl Kerényi*. Translated by Alexander Gelley. Ithaca, N.Y.: Cornell University Press, 1975.

Index

Amen Corner, The (James Baldwin), 6, 90
Anacreon, 90
Apollinaire, Guillaume, 87
Aristotle, 38
Aubrion, Michel, 51
Audiat, Pierre, 11
Austin, Everett, Jr., 3

Bachelard, Gaston, 49
Balzac, Honoré de, 6, 56
Baudelaire, Charles, 69, 85
Blot, Jean, 10, 12, 22, 40, 48, 65, 74, 83
Boisdeffre, Pierre de, 95

Caillois, Roger, 5
Callimachus, 90
Campanella, Tommaso, 48, 105n24
Canby, Vincent, 3
Cartier de Marchienne, Fernande de (Yourcenar's mother), 1. *See also* Works—Autobiography: *Labyrinthe du Monde, Le*
Cavafy, Constantin. *See* Works—Essays: "Présentation critique de Constantin Cavafy"
Champigny, Robert, 39–40
Charpentier, John, 23
Chateaubriand, François-René de, 53
Chenonceaux, Château de. *See* Works—Essays: "Ah, mon beau château"
Clouard, Henri, 57
Cocteau, Jean, 87
Colette, Sidonie, 5
Crayencour, Michel de (Yourcenar's father), 1. *See also* Works—Autobiography: *Labyrinthe du Monde, Le*
Crayencour, Marguerite de. *See* Yourcenar, Marguerite

Danse du loup, La (Serge Bramly), 97
Darbelnet, Jean, 88
Death of Vergil, The (Hermann Broch), 41
Delcroix, Maurice, 10, 51
Deroisin, Sophie, 56
Design and Truth in Autobiography (Roy Pascal), 66

Dichtung und Wahrheit (Wolfgang von Goethe), 66
Dimaras, Constantin, 88
Dorst, Jean, 5
Duchess of Langeais, The (Honoré de Balzac), 38
Dürer, Albrecht, 2

Eliade, Mircea, 54
Elissa Rhaïs (Paul Tabet), 97
Erasmus, Desiderius, 48
Euripides, 79, 81

Farrell, C. Frederick, Jr., and Farrell, Edith R., 59
Faulkner, William, 19
Fin de Raspoutine, La (Prince Felix Yousoupoff), 90
Flamel, Nicolas, 48, 51
Flaubert, Gustave, 6, 32
Fleishman, Avrom, 41
Flexner, Hortense, 88
Fontainas, André, 86
Foucault, Michel, 65–66
Freudian theories, 3, 35, 62, 64, 106n8
Frick, Grace, 4, 5

Galey, Matthieu, 6
Genette, Gérard, 40
Ghosts (Henrick Ibsen), 3
Gide, André, 9, 11
Giraudoux, Jean, 83
Giscard d'Estaing, Valéry (President of France), 5
Golding, William, 6
Goll, Claire, 27
Greco, El, 2, 6
Green, Julien, 5
Guitton, Jean, 90
Gusdorf, Georges, 69

Hell, Henri, 23
Henriot, Emile, 27
Historia Augusta. See Works—Essays: "Visages de l'Histoire dans *L'Histoire Auguste, Les*"

Homer, 90
Houville, Gérard d', 27
Howard, Richard, 88
Hugo, Victor, 20

I, Claudius (Robert Graves), 41
Ides of March, The (Thornton Wilder), 41
Ioannidi, Hélène, 88
Ionesco, Eugène, 5

Jaloux, Edmond, 11
Japanese nō, 78
Journal (André Gide), 93
Jung, Carl Gustav, 104n14

Kanters, Robert, 57
Kemp, Robert, 27
Kerényi, Karl, 27
Kohn, Ingeborg M., 92

Labyrinthe du Monde et le Paradis du coeur, Le (Jan Amos Comenius; adapted into French by Michel de Crayencour [Yourcenar's father]), 105n1
La Fayette, Mme de, 5
Lagerlöf, Selma. *See* Works—Essays: "Selma Lagerlöf, conteuse épique"
Lamartine, Alphonse de, 12
Laurencin, Marie, 87
Lebel, Maurice, 88
Lejeune, Philippe, 66
Little Mermaid, The (Hans Christian Andersen), 3, 78
Luccioni, Gennie, 56

Machiavelli, Niccolo, 29
Maeterlinck, Maurice, 2
"Mages, Les" (Victor Hugo), 93
Mann, Thomas, 27, 29. *See also* Works—Essays: "Humanisme et hermétisme chez Thomas Mann"
Marcel, Gabriel, 79, 83
Marius the Epicurian (Walter Pater), 41
Medici, Julian de', 57
Mendilow, A. A., 40
Mirandola, Pico della, 49
Mishima, Yukio, 6. *See also* Works—Essays: *Mishima ou la vision du Vide*
Mon coeur mis à nu (Charles Baudelaire), 65
Montaigne, Michel de, 19, 39, 70
Morand, Paul, 20
Murasaki, Lady, 21
My Truth (Indira Gandhi), 66

Name of the Rose, The (Umberto Eco), 97
Nietzsche, Friedrich, 51
Noailles, Anna de, 5
Noulet, Emilie, 86

Olney, James, 66
Onimus, Jean, 56
Orientales, Les (Victor Hugo), 12, 86
Ormesson, Jean d', 5

Paracelsus, Theophrastus, 43, 48
Pascal, Blaise, 51
Pindar, 2, 90, 91. *See also* Works—Essays: *Pindare*
Piranesi, Giambattista, 65. *See also* Works—Essays: "Cerveau noir de Piranèse, Le"
Polish Rider, The (Rembrandt), 24
Pollack, Jean, 90
Pritam, Amrita, 90
Proust, Marcel, 6, 41, 71

Rembrandt, 2, 6
Renza, Louis, 66
Republic, The (Plato), 34
Ricaumont, Jacques de, 93
Richelieu, Cardinal de, 5
Rilke, Rainer Maria, 10
Rimbaud, Arthur, 5, 71
Romains, Jules, 102n1
Rosbo, Patrick de, 52
Rubinstein, Lothar Henry, 80

Saint-Laurent, Yves, 5
Salammbô (Gustave Flaubert), 38
Sand, George, 5
Sappho, 90
Sartre, Jean-Paul, 100n2
Schlöndorff, Volker. *See* Works—Fiction: *Coup de Grâce* (film)
Scott, Walter, 56
Scudéry, Mlle de, 5
Si je mens (Françoise Giroud), 66
Soos, Emese, 51
Spender, Stephen, 3
Staël, Mme de, 5
Starobinski, Jean, 66
Steiner, George, 90
Styron, William, 70

Thérive, André, 27
Three Musketeers, The (Alexandre Dumas), 38
Toynbee, Arnold, 42
"Tradition and the Individual Talent" (T. S. Eliot), 39

Tragiques, Les (Agrippa d'Aubigné). *See* Works—Essays: *"Tragiques* d'Agrippa d'Aubigné, *Les"*
Truc, Gonzague, 56

Usurpation ou le roman de Marc Aurèle, L' (François Fontaine), 97

Valéry, Paul, 39, 66
Vergil, 11
Vier, Jacques, 36
View of Toledo (El Greco), 74
Vinci, Leonardo da, 48

Waves, The (Virginia Woolf), 3, 88. *See also* Works—Translations: *Vagues, Les*
What Maisie Knew (Henry James), 4, 88. *See also* Works—Translations: *Ce que savait Maisie*
Whatley, Janet, 33
Williams, Marion, 90
Woodbridge, Benjamin M., 5
Woolf, Virginia, 19

Yourcenar, Marguerite, adoption of pen name, 2; aristocratic origins, 1; becomes American citizen, 4; birth in Belgium, 1; close to fictional characters, 6–7; continues to write and publish, 5–6; contributes to expatriate journals, 3; death of father, 2; death of Grace Frick, 5; death of mother, 1; education, 1–2, 99n4; first works, 2; her influence, 97; honors and prizes, 5, 6; interest in social and political issues, 96, 108n16; literary awards, 4; moves permanently to Maine, 4; numerous works between 1951 and 1968, 4; part-time college instructor, 3; prefers simple country life, 4; refuses to be "woman writer," 96; residence in the United States, 3; residence on Aegean island, 2; serenity of mind, 6; suggested for Nobel Prize, 6; symbolist influences, 2; translation method, 109n37; translations, 3–4; tumultuous candidacy and election to French Academy, 5; travels, 2, 3, 4; visits to the United States, 3; works widely translated, 4; writes in different genres, 2, 3, 4, 5

WORKS—AUTOBIOGRAPHY:
Feux, 3, 58–62, 96
Labyrinthe du Monde, Le, 58, 65–71; *Archives du Nord*, 5, 65, 67, 70; *Quoi,*

l'Eternité?, 5; *Souvenirs pieux*, 5, 65, 67, 70
Songes et les sorts, Les, 3, 58, 62–65

WORKS—ESSAYS:
Mishima ou la vision du Vide, 6, 94–95
Pindare, 91–92
Sous bénéfice d'inventaire, 65, 92–94; "Ah, mon beau château," 92–93; "Cerveau noir de Piranèse, Le," 93; "Humanisme et hermétisme chez Thomas Mann," 94; "Présentation critique de Constantin Cavafy," 93–94; "Selma Lagerlöf, conteuse épique," 93; *"Tragiques* d'Agrippa d'Aubigné, *Les,"* 92; "Visages de L'Histoire dans *L'Histoire Auguste, Les,"* 92
Temps, ce grand sculpteur, Le, 6, 95
Tour de ma prison, Le, 97
Yeux ouverts, Les, 6, 95

WORKS—POETRY:
Charités d'Alcippe et autres poëmes, Les, 86–87
Dieux ne sont pas morts, Les, 2, 8, 85–86, 87
Jardin des chimères, Le, 2, 8, 84–85

WORKS—PROSE FICTION:
Alexis ou le traité du vain combat, 2, 8–11, 25
Comme l'eau qui coule, 6, 13, 72; *Anna, soror . . .* , 72–74, 96; "Belle Matinée, Une," 72, 76–77; "Homme obscur, Un," 72, 74–76
Coup de grâce, Le, 3, 23–26, 27, 96
Coup de Grâce (film by Volker Schlöndorff), 3
Denier du rêve, 3, 13–19, 37, 57, 65, 77, 78, 96
Mémoires d'Hadrien, 4, 8, 26, 27–42, 51, 55, 57, 65, 96
Mort conduit l'attelage, La, 2, 6, 13, 43, 72, 75; "D'après Dürer," 43, 72; "D'après Greco," 72, 107n3; "D'après Rembrandt," 72, 74, 76
Nouvelle Eurydice, La, 2, 11–13, 65, 96
Nouvelles orientales, 3, 20–23, 96; "Comment Wang-Fô fut sauvé," 20, 61; "Dernier Amour du Prince Genghi, Le," 21; "Fin de Marko Kraliévitch, La," 22; "Homme qui a aimé les Néréides, L'," 21; "Kâli décapitée," 21; "Lait de la mort, Le," 22; "Notre-Dame

des Hirondelles," 22; "Sourire de
Marko, Le," 20–21; "Tristesse de Cornélius Berg, La," 20; "Veuve Aphrodissia, La," 21–22
Oeuvre au noir, L', 3, 4, 13, 42, 43–57,
65, 72, 96
Oeuvres romanesque, 6

WORKS—THEATER:
Théâtre, 77; *Dialogue dans le marécage, Le*,
78–79; *Electre ou la chute des masques*,
79–81, 83, 96; *Mystère d'Alceste, Le*,

81–82, 83; *Petite Sirène, La*, 3, 78; *Qui
n'a pas son Minotaure?*, 67, 82–83;
Rendre à César, 3, 77–78, 101n20

WORKS—TRANSLATIONS:
Amen Corner, The (Le Coin des "Amen"), 6,
90
Blues et gospels, 6, 90
Ce que savait Maisie, 4, 88
Couronne et la lyre, La, 6, 90
Fleuve profond, sombre rivière, 3–4, 89, 96
Vagues, Les, 3, 88

848.914
Y 81

117 865

DATE DUE

DEMCO 38-297